# POTATOES

# POTATOES

65 delicious ways with the humble potato from fries to pies

## JENNY LINFORD

### PHOTOGRAPHY BY CLARE WINFIELD

RYLAND PETERS & SMALL
LONDON • NEW YORK

Dedication
For my father, who introduced
me to the joys of sautéed potatoes,
with my love.

Senior Designer  Sonya Nathoo
Designer  Emily Breen
Editor  Miriam Catley
Picture Researcher  Christina Borsi
Production  David Hearn
Art Director  Leslie Harrington
Editorial Director  Julia Charles
Publisher  Cindy Richards

Food stylists  Matthew Ford
 and Natalie Thomson
Prop Stylist  Olivia Wardle

Indexer  Vanessa Bird

First published in 2018
by Ryland Peters & Small
20–21 Jockey's Fields
London WC1R 4BW
and
341 E 116th St
New York NY 10029

www.rylandpeters.com

10 9 8 7 6 5 4 3 2 1

Text copyright © Jenny Linford 2018
Design and photographs copyright
© Ryland Peters & Small 2018

ISBN: 978-1-78879-028-4

Printed in China

A CIP record for this book is available
from the British Library. US Library
of Congress Cataloging-in-Publication
Data has been applied for.

Notes
• Both British (Metric) and
American (Imperial plus US cups)
ingredients measurements are
included in these recipes for your
convenience, however it is important
to work with one set of
measurements and not alternate
between the two within a recipe.
• All spoon measurements are level
unless otherwise specified.
• All eggs are medium (UK) or large
(US), unless specified as large, in
which case US extra-large should
be used. Uncooked or partially
cooked eggs should not be served
to the very old, frail, young children,
pregnant women or those with
compromised immune systems.

# CONTENTS

**6 INTRODUCTION**

**8 SUMMERY POTATOES**
History of the potato

**40 SUSTAINING POTATOES**
Potato varieties

**70 COMFORT POTATOES**
The cult of the chip

**102 SPICY POTATOES**
Culinary potatoes

**132 LUXURIOUS POTATOES**
Meet the potato farmers

**158 INDEX**
**160 ACKNOWLEDGEMENTS**

# INTRODUCTION

Modest in appearance, inexpensive and available throughout the year, the humble potato is today an everyday ingredient. Originally from South America, the potato was at first regarded with suspicion in the countries into which it was introduced as an exotic novelty. Over the centuries, however, it has become widely consumed and is now an important staple in many countries. Lower in calories than either bread or rice, it is also high in satiety and a useful source of fibre, potassium and Vitamin B6.

When one stops to think about it, a remarkable number of much-loved dishes feature the potato. To begin with, there are the ever-popular, irresistible chips or French fries – made by plunging chopped potatoes into hot fat – a perennial bestseller in fast food chains and upmarket restaurants alike. There are roast potatoes, cooked until golden-brown and crisp on the outside, yet soft within, an essential feature of a traditional Sunday roast lunch and also celebratory Christmas and Thanksgiving feasts. A well-made potato salad, dressed with smooth-textured mayonnaise or a tangy vinaigrette, punchy with cornichons and capers, is perfect summer eating, the ideal accompaniment to cold meats or poached salmon. Then, there's the potato gratin, a dish which sees thin slices of potato baked gently in a dish with a liquid – cream, milk or stock – softening and soaking

up flavour in the process. There are many variations on this gratin theme, including indulgent French versions and Sweden's rich Jansson's Temptation, all of which are fine examples of comfort food.

The potato, it turns out, is a very versatile ingredient, as the international range of recipes in this cookbook shows. Much human ingenuity has gone into devising interesting ways of cooking with it. In Indian cuisine, for example, spiced mashed potatoes are used to fill dosai (a type of pancake), chopped boiled potatoes are tossed with a spicy dressing for a street food dish and raw potato is coated with a chickpea flour batter and deep-fried to form a tasty snack. In Europe, potatoes add texture to an array of soups, are used raw and cooked to form dumplings and pancakes and fried in an imaginative number of ways. The fact that different potato cultivars offer waxy or floury textures adds to the variety of ways inventive cooks can use this vegetable.

There is, I feel, a friendly quality to the potato. It is one of the faithful ingredients that I always keep in stock in my kitchen cupboard. It is a familiar food, but one which is rightly regarded with deep affection in countries around the world.

# SUMMERY POTATOES

# HISTORY OF THE POTATO

Today the potato is one of the world's staple food crops, with both Asia and Europe producing over 80% of the global total. The origins of this starchy tuber are now known to be in the South American Andes, where it grew as a wild plant. By around 4,000BC – and possibly far earlier – the pre-Inca people of the region were cultivating potatoes. An ingenious way of preserving potatoes among Andean communities was a process which involved freezing, soaking and drying them, transforming them into a food called chuno which could then be safely stored for years.

It was the Spanish who, through their conquest of the Inca Empire in the sixteenth century, introduced this South American vegetable as an exotic novelty to Europe. Botanists classified it correctly as a member of the Solanaceae (nightshades) family. This strange new foodstuff which grew underground was initially

regarded with suspicion by people in Europe, thought to be unhealthy and linked to leprosy. Nicknames such as 'the devil's apple' or 'Eve's apple' reveal the ambiguity attached to it. In popular potato folklore, both Sir Francis Drake and Sir Walter Raleigh are credited with introducing the potato to England and Ireland, but historians are sceptical that this was the case.

The ruling classes in Europe saw the potential of this edible tuber as a useful food crop to feed a hungry population. In 1774 Frederick the Great of Prussia ordered the growing of potatoes by his citizens as a protection against famine. In France, the military pharmacist and agronomist Antoine-Augustin Parmentier (1737–1813) played a prominent part in popularizing the potato. Parmentier reputedly became accustomed to eating potatoes

when he was fed them as a prisoner of the Prussians during the Seven Years War and realised what a useful food they were. In France, however, the potato was regarded with suspicion and scorn as food for livestock, so Parmentier set to work converting French society partly through a range of imaginative publicity stunts. One story is that he persuaded Queen Marie Antoinette to wear potato flowers in her hair in order to popularize the crop. Another tale is that he cultivated a field of potatoes and caused it to be heavily guarded by soldiers during the day, which made people curious as to what this valuable crop could be and so they stole the plants from it by night. He also gave a famous dinner at Les Invalides for Benjamin Franklin in which the menu consisted entirely of potato dishes. Such was his campaigning that a number of potato dishes in French cuisine – Hachis Parmentier, Potage Parmentier – contain his name in tribute to his work.

Slowly the stigma against the potato ebbed away and by the 19th century the potato had become a staple food crop in countries across Europe. Indeed, so important had it become that it is seen as playing a key part in supporting Britain's population growth

during the Industrial Revolution. In Ireland, where the population doubled between 1780 and 1841, the high-yielding potato was an essential crop in sustaining an impoverished, rural community. Tragically, however, the arrival of potato blight in Ireland saw this vital crop fail, resulting in the Great Famine or the Great Hunger (1845–49) leading to the deaths of around a million Irish people and triggering mass emigration.

Today, the potato is considered the world's fourth most important food crop, after corn, wheat and rice. While it is a crop which performs best in temperate climates, it can be grown in sub-tropical and tropical climates. Historically, the highest levels of potato cultivation and consumption were in Europe and North America which saw the highest levels of potato cultivation and consumption. Recent decades, however, have seen countries in the developing world acquiring a taste for potatoes. Almost a third of potatoes produced are now cultivated in China and India. Its versatility as an ingredient means that it is used in a huge range of recipes – everything from French fries to Indian curries– a popular vegetable in kitchens around the globe.

# FRENCH POTATO SALAD

This classic potato salad benefits from having the vinaigrette added to the potatoes while they are still warm, as this means it soaks into the potatoes, giving a depth of flavour. A staple of summertime meals, serve it with cold meats such as salami or ham, or fish such as tuna or smoked salmon.

**500 g/17½ oz. even-sized waxy potatoes, peeled or scrubbed**
**3 tablespoons olive oil**
**2 tablespoons white wine vinegar**
**1 teaspoon Dijon mustard**
**2 teaspoons chopped capers**
**10 cornichons, finely chopped**
**1 spring onion/scallion, thinly sliced**
**salt and freshly ground black pepper**

SERVES 4

Cook the potatoes in boiling, salted water until tender; drain.

While the potatoes are cooking, make the dressing. Mix together the olive oil, vinegar and mustard by shaking them together in a clean, lidded jar to emulsify them. Season with salt and freshly ground black pepper.

As soon as the potatoes are cooked, cut in half or slices. Toss at once with the dressing, coating the potatoes evenly. Add in the capers, cornichons and spring onion/scallion. Serve while still warm or at room temperature. If making in advance, cover and chill, but bring to room temperature before serving.

# BLACK PEPPER CRISPS

There is a lightness and freshness to homemade crisps that makes them rather irresistible! The method is straightforward and the results very satisfying. Serve these with gin and tonics or chilled white wine for a pre-dinner party nibble.

**400 g/14 oz. potatoes**
**salt and freshly ground**
  **black pepper**
**oil, for deep-frying**

SERVES 4–6

Peel and slice the potatoes very thinly. Soak for 30 minutes in cold water, then drain and dry thoroughly.

Pour enough oil for deep-frying into a large, deep pan, to a depth of around half the pan. Heat the oil to 160°C (325°F).

Fry the potato slices in small batches, patting each batch dry thoroughly before adding to the oil. Fry the potato slices until they turn a deep golden colour, then remove with a slotted spoon and drain on paper towels. Season the freshly fried crisps at once with salt and plenty of freshly ground black pepper. Serve at once, or cool and store in an airtight container for up to three days.

# SWEDISH-STYLE HERRING AND POTATO SALAD

This pink-tinted, clean-tasting potato and beetroot/beet salad makes a pretty addition to a summer's buffet spread. It could also be enjoyed as part of a picnic or served for a light lunch on a hot sunny day.

500 g/17½ oz. waxy potatoes
2 cooked beetroot/beets, peeled and diced
100 g/3½ oz. herring fillets in dill marinade, drained and sliced into strips
½ red-skinned dessert apple, cored and thinly sliced

250 ml/1 cup plus 1 tablespoon soured/sour cream
15 g/½ cup chives, finely chopped
salt and freshly ground black pepper

SERVES 4

Cook the potatoes in boiling, salted water until tender; drain, peel and chop.

Mix together the potatoes, beetroot/beets, herring and apple. Add in the soured/sour cream and chives, reserving some of each for garnish, and gently but thoroughly mix together. Season with salt and freshly ground black pepper. Garnish with the reserved soured/sour cream and chives and a touch of freshly ground black pepper and chill before serving.

# CHORIZO POTATO SALAD

A Spanish-inspired potato salad, this dish is perfect for a light lunch on a hot summer's day, with a glass of chilled white wine or fino sherry.

500 g/17½ oz. waxy
  potatoes, peeled
2 tablespoons dry white
  wine
1 cooking chorizo, thinly
  sliced
2 tablespoons extra
  virgin olive oil
75 g/2¾ oz. jarred,
  marinated artichoke
  hearts, chopped
8 pimento-stuffed
  olives, sliced
2 preserved piquillo
  peppers, chopped
2 tablespoons freshly
  chopped parsley
salt and freshly ground
  black pepper

SERVES 4

Cook the potatoes in boiling, salted water until tender; drain. Place the hot potatoes in a bowl, pour over the white wine and set aside.

In a small frying pan/skillet, fry the chorizo over a low heat in its own fat, stirring often, until cooked through and lightly browned.

Slice the potatoes and toss with the olive oil. Add in the fried chorizo, artichoke hearts, olives, peppers and parsley, tossing well so that the potatoes take on the colour of the chorizo. Season with salt and freshly ground black pepper. Serve at room temperature.

# GRIDDLED TUNA NIÇOISE

When made with griddled fresh tuna, this classic French
salad becomes very elegant indeed. The combination of textures
and flavours is very pleasing, and this makes an excellent light lunch
for a hot summer's day.

2 tuna steaks
4 tablespoons extra
  virgin olive oil, plus
  extra for brushing
100 g/3½ oz. green
  beans, topped
500 g/17½ oz. new
  potatoes
2 tablespoons white
  wine vinegar
1 teaspoon grain
  mustard
1 shallot, finely chopped
1 lettuce heart, torn
8 cherry tomatoes,
  halved
2 eggs, hard-boiled/
  cooked, shelled and
  sliced into wedges
8 pitted black olives
salt and freshly ground
  black pepper
a handful of basil
  leaves, to garnish
  (optional)

SERVES 4

Season the tuna steaks with salt and freshly ground black pepper
and brush lightly on each side with olive oil.

Preheat a ridged griddle/grill pan until very hot. Cook the tuna steaks
on the griddle for 3 minutes on each side. Cool and cut into strips.

Cook the green beans in boiling water for 2–3 minutes until just
tender; drain and pat dry.

Cook the new potatoes in boiling, salted water until tender; drain
and slice. While the potatoes are cooking, make the dressing. Put
the 4 tablespoons of olive oil, the white wine vinegar and mustard
in a clean, lidded jar, cover and shake to mix well. Season the
dressing with salt and freshly ground black pepper.

Toss the warm potato slices with 2 tablespoons of the dressing and
the chopped shallot.

On a serving plate, layer the potato slices, green beans, lettuce,
cherry tomatoes, tuna strips, hard-boiled/cooked eggs and olives.
Pour over the remaining dressing, garnish with basil and serve.

# NEW POTATOES WITH MINT SALSA

Adding a sprig of fresh mint to new potatoes as they boil is a traditional way of cooking them in Britain and a lovely way of imparting a delicate, fragrant touch. Inspired by that classic flavour combination, this zesty, mint-based salsa dressing adds a vibrancy to firm-textured new potatoes, making them an excellent accompaniment to grilled/broiled fish or chicken.

500 g/17½ oz. small, even-sized new potatoes
40 fresh mint leaves
100 ml/⅓ cup olive oil
1 garlic clove, chopped
1 mild green chilli/chile, deseeded and chopped
grated zest and freshly squeezed juice of 2 limes
1 teaspoon salt

SERVES 4

Cook the potatoes in boiling, salted water until tender; drain.

Meanwhile, in a food processor, blend together the mint, olive oil, garlic, chilli/chile, lime zest and juice and the salt to form a salsa.

Drizzle the drained potatoes with the salsa and serve.

# POTATO RAITA

Yogurt-based raitas are a traditional, cooling accompaniment to spicy curries or tandoori chicken. This gentle dish is a great way of using up leftover boiled potatoes.

1 tablespoon ghee
or vegetable oil
8 fresh curry leaves,
shredded
1 teaspoon cumin
seeds
1 teaspoon black
mustard seeds
1 garlic clove, chopped
4 waxy potatoes,
peeled, boiled, cooled
and cubed
300 g/1½ cups Greek
or natural/plain yogurt
2 tablespoons freshly
chopped coriander/
cilantro
1 teaspoon paprika
grated zest of 1 lime
salt and freshly ground
black pepper

SERVES 4

Heat the ghee or vegetable oil in small frying pan/skillet over a medium heat. Add in the curry leaves and cumin and black mustard seeds and fry briefly, stirring, until fragrant.

Add in the garlic and fry, stirring, until it turns pale gold, taking care not to let it burn, as this will make it bitter. Remove from the heat and allow to cool.

Mix together the potatoes, yogurt and fried garlic mixture. Season with salt and freshly ground black pepper.

Top with the coriander/cilantro, paprika and lime zest and serve.

# MEDITERRANEAN MUSSEL POTATO SOUP

Inspired by the sunny flavours and ingredients of the Mediterranean – garlic, fresh herbs, tomatoes – this mussel and potato soup is a very cheerful dish. Serve it as a first course or for a light lunch.

1 kg/35 oz. mussels
50 ml/3½ tablespoons dry white wine
1 tablespoon olive oil
2 shallots, finely chopped
1 garlic clove, chopped
1 celery stalk, thinly sliced
1 bay leaf
1 sprig of thyme
1 x 400-g/14-oz. can chopped tomatoes
400 ml/1¾ cups fish stock
3 new potatoes, cut into 5 mm/¼ inch-thick slices
2 tablespoons freshly chopped parsley
2 teaspoons grated lemon zest
salt and freshly ground black pepper
crusty bread, to serve

SERVES 4

Rinse the mussels in cold water, discarding any that are open. Clean the closed mussels by pulling off their beards. Place the mussels in a large pan, add in 25 ml/1¾ tablespoons of the dry white wine. Cover and cook over a medium heat for 3–5 minutes until the mussels have opened. Drain the mussels, discarding any that haven't opened. Once cool enough to handle, remove the mussels from their shells and reserve.

Heat the olive oil in a large saucepan. Add in the shallots, garlic, celery, bay leaf and thyme. Fry gently, stirring, for 5 minutes. Add in the remaining white wine, bring to the boil and cook for 2 minutes. Add in the chopped tomatoes and cook for 2 minutes.

Add in the fish stock, season with salt and freshly ground black pepper and bring to the boil. Add in the potato slices and 1 tablespoon of the parsley. Simmer for 5–8 minutes until tender. Add in the reserved mussels and simmer for 2 minutes. Discard the bay leaf and thyme. Stir in the remaining parsley and the lemon zest and serve with crusty bread on the side.

# CHILLED LEEK AND POTATO SOUP

Slow, careful cooking transforms leeks and potatoes into a luxurious, French soup. The potatoes give a velvety texture, while the flavour is rich and full. Serve as a first course for a dinner party or lunch in the garden on a hot sunny day.

700 g/24½ oz. leeks
50 g/3½ tablespoons butter
200 g/7 oz. potatoes, peeled
 and cubed
50 ml/3½ tablespoons dry
 white wine
800 ml/3⅓ cups good chicken
 stock, ideally homemade
200 ml/¾ cup double/heavy
 cream, plus extra to garnish

freshly grated nutmeg
salt and freshly ground black
 pepper
freshly chopped chives,
 to garnish
croûtons, to serve (optional)

SERVES 4

Trim the leeks, discarding their tough outer casing and dark green tops. Finely chop and rinse thoroughly to get rid of any soil trapped between the layers.

Melt the butter in a large, heavy-based saucepan over a low heat. Add in the leeks and fry very gently for 10 minutes, stirring often so as to prevent them from scorching.

Add in the cubed potatoes, mixing well. Pour in the wine, increase the heat to medium, and cook for a few minutes, stirring now and then, until most of the wine has evaporated. Add in the chicken stock and season with salt and freshly ground black pepper.

Bring to the boil, reduce the heat and simmer for 25 minutes, until the potatoes are tender.

Blend the soup thoroughly until smooth, then stir in the cream and season with freshly grated nutmeg. Cool and chill.

Serve chilled, with each portion garnished with a swirl of cream, a sprinkling of chives and freshly ground black pepper, and croûtons, if desired.

# GADO-GADO

A classic Indonesian dish, this textured, vegetarian salad is topped with a distinctive salty-sweet, spicy peanut sauce, which is addictively tasty! Serve for a light meal or as part of an Indonesian feast. For a vegan version, simply omit the hard-boiled/cooked eggs.

6 waxy potatoes, boiled and halved
½ cucumber, sliced
100 g/3½ oz. sugar snap peas or mangetout/snow peas, halved
100 g/3½ oz. baby sweetcorn, halved lengthways
3 hard-boiled/cooked eggs, shelled and halved
fresh coriander/cilantro sprigs, to serve (optional)

GADO-GADO SAUCE
2 lemongrass stalks
1 onion, finely chopped
1 garlic clove, chopped
½ teaspoon chilli/chili powder
½ teaspoon ground turmeric
4 tablespoons vegetable or sunflower oil
200 ml/¾ cup canned coconut milk
4 tablespoons dark brown soft/packed sugar
100 g/¾ cup roasted peanuts, finely ground
freshly squeezed juice of ½ lemon
salt

SERVES 4

First make the gado-gado sauce. Peel off the tough outer casing from the lemongrass stalks. Finely chop the white, bulbous part of each stalk, discarding the fibrous remainder.

Blend together the chopped lemongrass, onion, garlic, chilli/chili powder and turmeric into a rough paste.

Heat the oil in a wok until hot. Add in the lemongrass paste and fry over a medium heat, stirring often, for 5 minutes, until fragrant. Stir in the coconut milk and sugar and cook gently over a low heat, stirring now and then, for a further 5 minutes. Add in the ground peanuts and simmer, stirring, for a further 5 minutes. Stir in the lemon juice and season with salt. Set aside to cool.

To serve the gado-gado, put the cold potatoes in a serving dish and top with the cucumber, sugar snap peas or mangetout/snow peas and baby sweetcorn. Plate up the gado-gado and pour over the sauce. Top with the cold hard-boiled/cooked egg halves and serve with a sprig of coriander/cilantro, if desired.

# PESTO, POTATO AND GREEN BEAN LINGUINE

This appealing pasta, potato and green bean dish is a classic of Genoa in Italy, from where pesto is said to have originated. Making your own pesto from fresh basil, olive oil and pine nuts/kernels is quick and easy, and the results are fragrant and delicious.

400 g/14 oz. linguine or trenette
200 g/7 oz. waxy potatoes, peeled and diced
100 g/3½ oz. green beans, topped, tailed and cut into 3-cm/1-inch pieces
salt and freshly ground black pepper

PESTO
50 g/⅓ cup pine nuts/kernels
50 g/1¾ oz. basil leaves
1 garlic clove, crushed
a pinch of salt
100 ml/⅓ cup extra virgin olive oil
50 g/⅔ cup grated Parmesan cheese, plus extra to serve

SERVES 4

First, make the pesto. Lightly toast the pine nuts/kernels in a dry frying pan/skillet; allow to cool. In a food processor, blend together the toasted pine nuts/kernels, basil, garlic, salt and olive oil to form a textured paste. Mix in the Parmesan cheese. Set aside.

Bring a large pan of salted water to the boil. Add in the linguine or trenette and cook until al dente. Meanwhile, in a separate pan, cook the potato chunks in boiling, salted water until tender; drain. In a third pan, cook the green beans in boiling water until al dente; drain.

Drain the linguine and toss with the pesto, coating well. Add in the potato chunks and green beans and toss together. Serve at once with extra grated Parmesan cheese and freshly ground black pepper.

# SPANISH POTATO TORTILLA

There is something very satisfying about this quintessentially
Spanish dish. Through careful cooking, a few simple ingredients
– eggs, potatoes, onions and olive oil – are ingeniously transformed
into a favourite tapas dish.

250 ml/1 cup plus
  1 tablespoon olive oil
300 g/10½ oz. waxy
  potatoes, peeled,
  quartered and thinly
  sliced
1 onion, halved and
  thinly sliced
6 large eggs
salt and freshly ground
  black pepper

SERVES 4–6 AS PART OF
A TAPAS SPREAD, OR 2
FOR A MEAL

Pour the olive oil into a small, heavy-based frying pan/skillet with
a 16-cm/6¼-inch base. Add in the sliced potatoes and onion,
cover the pan and cook gently over a low heat until softened but
not coloured, stirring now and then. In effect, you're stewing the
vegetables in the oil.

While the potatoes are cooking, beat together the eggs in a large bowl
and season with salt and freshly ground black pepper.

Strain the potato mixture into a colander, reserving the olive oil for
future use. Season the potato mixture lightly with salt and pour the
hot vegetables into the beaten eggs, gently mixing together.

Heat 1 tablespoon of the reserved oil in the same frying pan/skillet.
Add in the egg mixture and fry gently for 10–15 minutes until it has
set and there is just a small pool of liquid egg on the surface.

Cover the frying pan/skillet with a plate that is larger than the pan
and tip over the frying pan/skillet so as to invert the tortilla onto the
plate. Gently slide the tortilla back into the frying pan/skillet and cook
for a further 2 minutes to set the other side. Remove from the pan
and serve warm or at room temperature.

# SALMON FISHCAKES WITH WATERCRESS SAUCE

Home-made fishcakes make an appealing light lunch or dinner. This recipe uses cooked fresh salmon, but you can easily substitute other fish such as smoked haddock or canned tuna to good effect.

500 g/17½ oz.
  potatoes, peeled
  and chopped
2 spring onions/
  scallions, finely
  chopped
25 g/1½
  tablespoons butter
1 tablespoon milk
freshly grated nutmeg
500 g/17½ oz.
  cooked skinless
  salmon fillet, flaked
grated zest of
  1 lemon
salt and freshly
  ground black
  pepper
vegetable or
  sunflower oil, for
  shallow-frying
lemon wedges,
  to serve
watercress, to serve

COATING
1 egg, beaten
fine matzo meal or
  dry breadcrumbs,
  for coating

WATERCRESS SAUCE
100 g/3½ oz.
  watercress, roughly
  chopped
freshly squeezed juice
  of ½ lemon
4 tablespoons
  mayonnaise
1 tablespoon dry
  white wine
1 teaspoon Dijon
  mustard

SERVES 4

Cook the potatoes in boiling, salted water until tender; drain. While the potatoes are cooking, fry the spring onions/scallions in the butter until softened. Add the fried spring onions/scallions with the butter and the milk to the potatoes and mash well. Season with freshly ground black pepper and freshly grated nutmeg and allow to cool.

Make the watercress sauce by blending together the watercress and lemon juice into a purée. Mix this into the mayonnaise, then stir in the wine and mustard. Season with salt and freshly ground black pepper. Set aside.

Mix the flaked salmon and lemon zest into the mashed potato mixture. Shape into eight fishcakes. For coating dip each fishcake first into the beaten egg, then coat in matzo meal or breadcrumbs.

Heat the oil in a large frying pan/skillet and fry the fishcakes for 5 minutes on each side, until golden brown. Serve hot or at room temperature with the Watercress Sauce, lemon wedges, a handful of watercress and some chips/fries.

# HARISSA POTATO AND LENTIL SALAD

The combination of subtly piquant, crispy fried potatoes with the earthy lentils makes this a very satisfying dish. Serve it for a vegan meal or as a side dish for barbecued lamb or chicken.

100 g/²⁄₃ cup Puy or brown lentils

2 tablespoons extra virgin olive oil

1 teaspoon freshly squeezed lemon juice

400 g/14 oz. waxy potatoes, peeled and finely diced

1 red onion, finely chopped

1–2 teaspoons harissa paste

salt and freshly ground black pepper

sunflower oil, for shallow-frying

chopped coriander/cilantro leaves, to garnish

SERVES 4

Rinse the lentils, drain and place in a large pan. Cover generously with water and bring to the boil. Reduce the heat and simmer for 20 minutes until the lentils are tender but retain some texture, then drain.

Dress the lentils with the olive oil and lemon juice, seasoning well with salt and freshly ground black pepper. Place in a serving dish.

Pour enough sunflower oil into a large frying pan/skillet so that it forms a shallow layer across the surface of the pan and heat up. Add in the diced potatoes and fry, stirring now and then, until golden brown on all sides.

Add in the onion and fry for 2–3 minutes until softened. Mix in the harissa paste, coating the fried potatoes, and fry, stirring, for 2 minutes.

Mix the harissa potatoes with the lentils, sprinkle with coriander/cilantro leaves and serve.

# SUSTAINING POTATOES

# POTATO VARIETIES

When asked to name potato varieties, most of us would be able to come up just with a handful of names. In fact, there are thousands of potato varieties. Appropriately, potato diversity is at its richest in the Andean highlands of Peru, Bolivia and Ecuador, the part of the world where the potato originated from and was first cultivated. In this region alone, thousands of potato varieties are grown. The diversity of these Andean potatoes is striking: their skins are coloured yellow, pink, red, purple and black while shapes range from long, thin and smooth, resembling fingers, to round and knobbly. The flesh inside, too, ranges in colour from the pale white of the Papa Blanca to the deep purple-red of the Yawar, a Quecha word for 'blood'. Given this level of variety, it is appropriate that the International Potato Center, a research facility working on potatoes and other tubers as an important food source for the future, is based in Peru. Today, farmers around the world face challenges on a number of fronts; climate change and extreme weather being one, and plant pests and diseases, which in our connected modern world can spread rapidly throughout the globe. The danger of becoming dependent on one genetically uniform crop was tragically demonstrated in the nineteenth century by Ireland's Great Hunger, during which the potato crop on which many people in the country depended for food – a variety called Lumper which produced good yields in poor soil – succumbed to blight with tragic consequences for millions. Many of these Andean potato varieties are notably hardy because of the environment in which they grow, so researchers are excited by their potential usefulness to agriculture globally.

Quecha Potato Field

From a cook's point of view, one useful way of categorizing potatoes is by their texture when cooked. Potatoes vary in their starch content and this affects how they respond to cooking techniques. The type of potatoes that have a high starch content are known as 'floury' or 'mealy'. These lend themselves to cooking techniques such as baking, roasting, deep-frying or mashing, producing light, fluffy results. In contrast, potatoes with a low starch content, known as 'waxy' potatoes, hold their shape and retain a firmness of texture, so are excellent for boiling or steaming, working well in gratins and ideal for salads. What are known as 'all-purpose' potatoes fall in between the two extremes, possessing a medium starch content which allows them to be used for a number of cooking methods, such as baking or mashing.

Around the world, certain varieties are particularly esteemed, among them Jersey Royals. Potatoes feature in a number of classic recipes in French cuisine, from Potato Dauphinoise to sautéed potatoes. Among the potato varieties esteemed in France is La Ratte, a small, waxy potato with a creamy texture and a nutty flavour. Originally grown in the nineteenth century, it fell out of favour, but was reintroduced in the 1980s and enjoyed much popularity among chefs. When the legendary chef Joel Robuchon used La Ratte to make his renowned purée, the potato's culinary cachet was ensured. Such is the demand for it among restaurants and food cognoscenti, that La Ratte is also grown in other countries, including the US. Another French gourmet cultivar is the Vitelotte, a distinctive waxy potato with purple skin and flesh, cultivated since the early 1800s. In Britain, a number of potatoes are popular, among them the King Edward. Easy to recognise thanks to its golden skin patched with pink, this is a floury potato, so excellent for roasting and baking.

It was cultivated in 1902, the year of Edward VII's coronation, hence its regal name, and is one of Europe's oldest potato varieties still being grown commercially. In America, the Russet Burbank is a widely used mealy potato cultivar, which traces its origins back to the early years of the twentieth century. Yukon Gold, with its distinctive yellow-coloured flesh, is another popular American variety, dating from the 1960s, and classified as an 'all-purpose' potato. In Germany, a popular example of a waxy potato is the Annabelle variety, noted for its slightly sweet flavour and firm, creamy texture.

Seek out heritage/heirloom varieties at food shops or markets or farmers' markets, (which link food producers directly with their customers). The diverse world of the potato is well worth exploring and much good eating is offered en-route!

# SAUTÉED POTATOES WITH PANCETTA AND GARLIC

This is definitely a dish for garlic-lovers! Frying the potatoes with garlic instead of onion adds a rich umami tastiness to this classic potato dish. Serve it with poached or fried eggs for a substantial breakfast or a light lunch.

500 g/17½ oz. waxy
    potatoes
12 garlic cloves
100 g/3½ oz. pancetta,
    cut into short strips
1 tablespoon olive oil
salt and freshly ground
    black pepper
2 tablespoons freshly
    chopped parsley

SERVES 4

Cook the potatoes in boiling, salted water until tender. Drain and cut into 5-mm/¼-inch-thick slices.

Blanch the garlic cloves in a separate small pan of boiling water for 5 minutes, until tender; drain and peel.

Fry the pancetta in a heavy-based frying pan/skillet over a medium heat for 2–3 minutes. Add in the olive oil, heat through and then add in the potato slices. Fry, stirring often, for 5–7 minutes until the potato slices are golden brown on both sides.

Add in the peeled garlic cloves and fry for 2–3 minutes until lightly golden. Season with salt and freshly ground black pepper. Sprinkle with the parsley and serve at once.

# HERBED CRUSHED POTATOES

Crushing potatoes is a very easy way of preparing them, as no peeling is required! The roughly crushed potatoes soak up the flavours of the dressing, while the use of lemon zest and herbs give a real lift to the dish. Serve with baked salmon, baked chicken thighs or grilled/broiled lamb chops for an easy meal.

500 g/17½ oz.
  even-sized waxy
  potatoes
2 tablespoons extra
  virgin olive oil
grated zest of ½ lemon
1 teaspoon freshly
  squeezed lemon juice
2 tablespoons freshly
  chopped chives
2 tablespoons freshly
  chopped mint leaves
3 tablespoons finely
  chopped parsley
salt and freshly ground
  black pepper

SERVES 4

Cook the potatoes in boiling, salted water until tender; drain.

Return the potatoes to the pan. Use a masher to roughly crush them, making sure not to totally mash them.

Add in the olive oil, lemon zest and juice and season with salt and freshly ground black pepper, mixing well. Add the chives, mint and parsley and mix in. Serve warm or at room temperature.

# SEAWEED BUTTER POTATOES

The salty flavour of the seaweed together with the nuttiness
of steamed potatoes works a treat. Serve as an elegant accompaniment
to a whole baked seabass or salmon.

**1 small handful of dried
wakame seaweed**
**1 small handful of dried
arame or dulse
seaweed**
**700 g/24½ oz.
even-sized waxy
potatoes**
**½ sheet of nori
seaweed, finely
chopped**
**25 g/1½ tablespoons
butter, softened**

SERVES 4

First, rehydrate two of the seaweeds to soften them. Soak the
wakame in tepid water for 10 minutes, then drain. Soak the arame
or dulse in tepid water for 5 minutes, then drain.

Steam or boil the potatoes until tender; drain.

While the potatoes are cooking, use a fork to mash the pieces of nori
seaweed into the butter, mixing well.

Place the freshly cooked potatoes at once into a serving bowl.
Dot with the nori butter, so that it melts and coats them, then top the
potatoes with the wakame and arame seaweeds. Serve at once.

# CALDO VERDE

This rustic Portuguese soup is substantial enough to serve as a meal in its own right. Serve with a few slices of chorizo on the top and some fresh bread on the side.

1 tablespoon extra virgin olive oil, plus extra for serving
1 onion, chopped
1 garlic clove, chopped
400 g/14 oz. floury potatoes, peeled and chopped
600 ml/2½ cups chicken or vegetable stock
150 g/3 cups kale
1 cooking chorizo, finely sliced (optional)
salt and freshly ground black pepper
rustic bread, to serve

SERVES 4

Heat the olive oil in a large saucepan. Gently fry the onion and garlic, stirring often so as to prevent them from burning, for 2 minutes, until the onion and garlic have softened.

Add in the potatoes and stock and season with salt and freshly ground black pepper. Bring to the boil, reduce the heat, cover and simmer for 15 minutes.

Tear the leaves off the kale, discarding the tough stalks. Roll up the leaves tightly and slice them as thinly as possible into shreds. Alternatively, chop the kale into thick ribbons.

Remove the simmered soup from the heat and roughly mash the softened potatoes into the soup, leaving some chunks.

Return the soup to the hob/stovetop, bring to the boil and add in the kale. Simmer for 2–3 minutes until the kale is just tender.

Meanwhile, fry the chorizo slices (if using) in a frying pan/skillet until cooked through and lightly browned.

When made the traditional way with very finely chopped kale, this simple soup has a satisfying texture making it a pleasure to eat. Serve each portion of soup with a few chorizo slices (if using) on top, some freshly ground black pepper, a splash of extra virgin olive oil.

# BOULANGÈRE POTATOES

This classic French way of cooking potatoes gives them a wonderful, savoury depth of flavour. It is a simple dish, requiring very little work from the cook apart from the slicing. It cooks slowly and gently in the oven and is a traditional accompaniment to roast meat such as lamb or beef.

40 g/3 tablespoons
butter
1 onion, halved and
thinly sliced
1 bay leaf
1 kg/35 oz. potatoes,
peeled and sliced
widthways into
2–5-mm/$^1$/$_{16}$–$^1$/$_4$-inch
thick slices
400 ml/1$^3$/$_4$ cups beef
or chicken stock
salt and freshly ground
black pepper

SERVES 6

Preheat the oven to 200°C (400°F) Gas 6.

Heat 20 g/1½ tablespoons of the butter in a frying pan/skillet. Fry the onion with the bay leaf, stirring now and then, over a low heat until the onion is well softened and lightly browned.

Layer half the fried onion in the base of a shallow, ovenproof dish and discard the bay leaf. Season the potato slices well with salt and freshly ground black pepper. Arrange half the potato slices over the onion, then layer the potato slices with the remaining fried onion. Top with the remaining potato slices.

Bring the stock to the boil in a saucepan. Pour the hot stock into the dish over the potato and onion layers. Dot with the remaining butter.

Bake in the preheated oven for 1–1¼ hours until the potatoes are tender and the top is golden brown. Serve at once.

# POTATO CHEESE SCONES

Floury potatoes give a delightfully light texture to these traditional savoury scones, best eaten hot from the pan, topped with cold butter. Serve for breakfast or a tea-time treat.

450 g/15¾ oz. floury potatoes, peeled and chopped

25 g/1½ tablespoons butter

50 g/½ cup grated Cheddar cheese

25 g/⅓ cup grated Parmesan cheese

75 g/½ cup self-raising/rising flour, plus extra for dusting

salt and freshly ground black pepper

butter, to serve

MAKES 24 SCONES

Cook the potatoes in boiling, salted water until tender; drain and transfer to a bowl. Add in the butter, Cheddar and Parmesan and mash together well.

Stir in the flour to form a soft dough. Season with salt and freshly ground black pepper.

On a lightly floured surface, pat out the dough to 1 cm/½ inch thickness. Cut into 24 triangles.

Preheat a large, heavy-based frying pan/skillet or griddle/grill pan until very hot. Add in the potato triangles, cooking them in two batches. Fry the potato scones for 3 minutes on each side, until browned on both sides. Serve at once with butter.

# CHICKPEA, CHARD AND POTATO STEW

This is a homely, nourishing one-pot meal. The potatoes soak up the stock, becoming tasty and tender, contrasting well with the nutty chickpeas and the chard. Dried chickpeas have a better texture, but if time is short you can substitute a can of chickpeas in water, rinsing them and adding them in after the potatoes have simmered for 10 minutes.

120 g/¾ cup dried chickpeas, soaked overnight
2 tablespoons olive oil
1 onion, chopped
1 celery stalk, thinly sliced
1 red (bell) pepper, deseeded and chopped into short strips
1 teaspoon sweet smoked pimentón or paprika
a splash of dry white wine
300 g/10½ oz. waxy potatoes, quartered
400 ml/1¾ cups chicken or vegetable stock
200 g/7 oz. chard or spinach, shredded
1 tablespoon chopped preserved lemon (optional)
salt and freshly ground black pepper

SERVES 4

Drain the soaked chickpeas. Bring a large pan of water to the boil, add in the chickpeas and cook for around 1–1½ hours, until they are tender but retain some texture; drain.

Heat the olive oil in a frying pan/skillet. Add in the onion and fry gently over a low heat for 5 minutes, stirring often. Add in the celery and red (bell) pepper and fry for a further 3 minutes.

Sprinkle over the pimentón and add in the white wine. Cook briefly, stirring, then add in the potatoes and stock. Season with salt and freshly ground black pepper.

Bring to the boil, cover, reduce the heat and simmer for 20 minutes until the potatoes are tender.

Add in the chard or spinach and the cooked chickpeas, mixing well. Cover and cook for 5 minutes, until the chard has wilted and softened. Mix in the preserved lemon (if using) and serve at once.

# GARDENER'S PIE

This vegetarian take on a meat-based Shepherd's Pie is ideal for a simple, hearty midweek meal. Serve it with green beans, broccoli or peas on the side.

1 tablespoon olive oil
1 onion, chopped
1 garlic clove, chopped
1 celery stalk, thinly sliced
1 red (bell) pepper, deseeded and finely chopped
200 g/3 cups mushrooms, thickly sliced
1 tablespoon tomato purée/paste
1 x 400-g/14-oz. can chopped tomatoes
a pinch of dried oregano
1 x 400-g/14-oz. can borlotti beans in water, drained and rinsed
1 x 400-g/14-oz. can butter/lima beans in water, drained and rinsed
2 tablespoons freshly chopped parsley
900 g/2 lbs. potatoes, peeled and chopped into chunks
25 g/1½ tablespoons butter
splash of milk
2 teaspoons grain mustard
25 g/¼ cup grated Cheddar cheese
salt and freshly ground black pepper

SERVES 4-6

Preheat the oven to 200°C (400°F) Gas 6.

Heat the olive oil in a large frying pan/skillet. Fry the onion gently for 3 minutes, stirring now and then, until softened. Add in the garlic, celery and red (bell) pepper and fry until just softened. Add the mushrooms and fry, stirring, until they are lightly coloured.

Mix in the tomato purée/paste, then the chopped tomatoes. Season with the oregano and salt and freshly ground black pepper. Bring to the boil, then reduce the heat and simmer for 5 minutes. Add in the borlotti and butter/lima beans and the parsley. Cook for a further 5 minutes.

Meanwhile, cook the potatoes in boiling, salted water until tender; drain. Mash the potatoes with the butter and milk, seasoning with freshly ground black pepper. Mix in the mustard thoroughly.

Place the bean mixture in an ovenproof dish. Top with the mustard mash, spreading it in an even layer. Use a fork to texture the mash and then sprinkle with the Cheddar cheese. Bake in the preheated oven for 30 minutes until heated through and the cheese has melted. Serve at once.

# MISO POTATO SOUP

Japanese miso paste adds an umami richness to this textured potato soup. Serve it as a tasty first course or enjoy it on its own for a light lunch.

1½ tablespoons vegetable or sunflower oil

1 leek, washed and thinly sliced

700 g/24½ oz. floury potatoes, peeled and diced

1 tablespoon Amontillado sherry

1 heaped tablespoon brown miso paste

1 litre/quart chicken or vegetable stock

1 teaspoon soy sauce

200 g/3 cups brown closed cap mushrooms, thickly sliced

1 tablespoon freshly chopped chives

salt and freshly ground black pepper

SERVES 4

Heat 1 tablespoon of the oil in a large saucepan over a medium heat. Add in the leek and fry, stirring, until softened. Add the potatoes and mix well. Add the sherry and cook for 1–2 minutes. Mix in the miso paste.

Pour in the stock and add the soy sauce. Bring to the boil, cover and simmer for 20 minutes until the potatoes have softened. Taste the soup and adjust the seasoning as required with the salt and freshly ground black pepper.

Remove half the soup and blend it until smooth using a stick blender or a jug blender. Return the blended soup to the pan and mix with the remaining soup. Simmer gently to heat through.

Meanwhile, heat the remaining oil in a frying pan/skillet. Fry the mushrooms until lightly browned. Mix them into the soup. Garnish with the chives and serve at once.

# STOVED CHICKEN

This homely chicken and potato dish is comfort food at its best.
The soft potatoes soak up the stock in the most delicious way, making
it a hearty and satisfying dish. Serve with a side vegetable such as
buttered cabbage, broccoli or glazed carrots.

2 onions, sliced

2 bacon rashers/slices, cut into strips

2 sprigs of thyme

2 tablespoons olive oil

40 g/3 tablespoons butter

8 chicken thighs, skin on

700 g/24½ oz. potatoes, peeled and thinly sliced

300 ml/1¼ cups chicken stock

salt and freshly ground black pepper

SERVES 4

Preheat the oven to 200°C (400°F) Gas 6.

Fry the onions, bacon and thyme in 1 tablespoon of the olive oil in
a frying pan/skillet until the onion is softened and the bacon cooked.

Heat 20 g/1½ tablespoons of the butter in a separate large frying
pan/skillet. Add the chicken thighs and fry until golden brown on both
sides. Season with salt and freshly ground black pepper.

Toss the potato slices with the remaining olive oil and season with
salt and freshly ground black pepper. Mix together with the fried
onion mixture.

Layer half the potato mixture in an ovenproof casserole dish. Top
with the fried chicken and finish off with a layer of the remaining
potato mixture.

Bring the stock to the boil in a small pan and pour over the potatoes
in the casserole dish. Bring the stock back to the boil, cover tightly
and transfer the casserole into the preheated oven to bake for 1 hour.

Preheat the grill/broiler to high. Uncover the casserole dish, dot with
the remaining butter and grill/broil until the potatoes are browned.
Serve at once.

# MUSHROOM BACON POTATO DUMPLINGS

Making these filled dumplings is a very satisfying thing to do. The contrast between the soft potato casing and the savoury filling works a treat, especially when served with sweet lingonberry jam/jelly. Ideal for cold weather, this makes a warming, heartening meal.

1 kg/35 oz. floury
  potatoes
1 egg and 1 egg yolk,
  beaten
25 g/3 tablespoons
  plain/all-purpose flour
freshly grated nutmeg
salt and freshly ground
  black pepper
50 g/3½ tablespoons
  butter, melted, to
  serve
freshly chopped chives
  or parsley, to garnish
lingonberry jam/jelly
  or redcurrant jelly,
  to serve

MUSHROOM AND
BACON FILLING
1½ tablespoons
  vegetable or sunflower
  oil
½ large onion, finely
  chopped
2 rashers/slices of
  bacon, finely chopped
115 g/1¾ cups
  mushrooms, finely
  chopped

SERVES 8

Boil the unpeeled potatoes until tender. Drain and, while they are still hot, peel them at once and mash very well, ensuring there are no lumps. Add in the beaten egg mixture and flour and mix thoroughly. Season well with salt and freshly grated nutmeg. Mix together to form a soft dough.

Shape the dough into four even-sized logs, around 4 cm/1½ inches across. Cover and chill in the fridge for 30 minutes.

While the dough is chilling, make the mushroom and bacon filling. Heat the oil in a frying pan/skillet, add in the onion and fry gently, stirring often, until softened. Add in the bacon and mushrooms and fry, stirring often, until the bacon and mushrooms are cooked. Season with salt, bearing in mind the saltiness of the bacon, and freshly ground black pepper. Set aside.

Cut each potato dough log into four even-sized portions. To form a dumpling, take one portion, push a hole in the centre with your thumb and fill with a teaspoon of the mushroom and bacon filling. Pinch the dough together over the filling to seal it well. Repeat the process until all the potato dough portions and filling have been used. Cover and chill for 30 minutes before cooking in order to allow the dough to firm up.

Bring a large pan of water to a simmering boil. Cook the dumplings in batches, adding them very gently to the water and cooking over a low heat for 10 minutes, without letting the water come to the boil. Remove carefully with a slotted spoon and drain.

Serve the freshly cooked dumplings with melted butter spooned over them, a sprinkling of chives or parsley, freshly ground black pepper and lingonberry jam/jelly or redcurrant jelly on the side.

# CHEESY THREE-ROOT BAKE

Cheese and potatoes are one of those simple but satisfying combinations. This homely dish makes an excellent mid-week supper. Serve it on its own for a vegetarian meal or accompany it with grilled/broiled bacon or sausages.

500 g/17½ oz. waxy potatoes, peeled
2 carrots, peeled
200 g/7 oz. celeriac/celery root, peeled and cut into chunks
30 g/2 tablespoons butter
1 leek, washed and chopped
2 tablespoons plain/all-purpose flour
300 ml/1¼ cups milk
100 g/1 cup grated Cheddar cheese
2 tablespoons breadcrumbs
salt and freshly ground black pepper

SERVES 4

Cook the potatoes, carrots and celeriac/celery root in boiling, salted water until tender; drain. Slice the potatoes, carrots and celeriac/celery root.

Preheat the oven to 200°C (400°F) Gas 6.

Melt the butter in a heavy-based saucepan. Add in the leek and fry gently over a low heat, stirring, until softened. Mix in the flour and fry, stirring, for 2 minutes. Gradually mix in the milk, stirring as you do so. Bring to the boil, stirring, so that it thickens into a white sauce. Stir in 75 g/¾ cup of the cheese until melted and season with salt and freshly ground black pepper.

Place the root vegetables in an ovenproof baking dish. Pour over the cheese sauce and mix gently, so that the vegetables are coated. Sprinkle with the remaining cheese and the breadcrumbs.

Bake in the preheated oven for 30 minutes until golden brown. Serve at once.

# BAKED SEABASS ON HERBED POTATOES

This impressive-looking fish dish is simple to cook, making it a perfect dinner party dish. The combination of the moist, delicate seabass flesh and fragrant herbed potatoes means that it tastes as good as it looks.

400 g/14 oz. waxy potatoes, cut into 5-mm/¼-inch slices
2 tablespoons olive oil
1 shallot, finely chopped
2 tablespoons freshly chopped tarragon leaves
1 tablespoon freshly chopped parsley
grated zest of 1 lemon, reserving a little to garnish
2 seabass (roughly 700 g/24½ oz.), cleaned
6 lemon slices
4 sprigs of tarragon
100 ml/⅓ cup dry white wine
salt and freshly ground black pepper

SERVES 4

Preheat the oven to 200°C (400°F) Gas 6.

Bring a pan of salted water to the boil. Add in the potato slices, cook for 5 minutes, then drain. Toss the potato slices with the olive oil and season with salt and freshly ground black pepper.

Layer the potato slices in a roasting pan, tossing with the shallot, chopped tarragon and parsley. Sprinkle with the lemon zest.

Season the seabass with salt and freshly ground black pepper. Cut three slashes in each side of each fish. Place the lemon slices and tarragon sprigs in the cavities.

Place the seabass on top of the potato mixture. Pour over the wine. Bake in the preheated oven for 40 minutes until the fish is cooked through and the potatoes are slightly crisped. Serve at once.

# COMFORT POTATOES

# THE CULT OF THE CHIP

Our love affair with chips or French fries, as the Americans call them, shows no signs of abating. There is something very tempting about those slivers of potato, deep-fried in oil until golden-brown, offering a pleasurable contrast between the crisp coating and the soft interior. Indeed, is there anyone who has not 'stolen' a chip from someone else's plate?! Chips play an integral part in a number of iconic dishes from around the world: Britain's fish and chips, America's burgers and fries, France's steak frites, Germany's currywurst and frites, Belgium's moules frites and Canada's poutine. Condiments eaten with chips range from Britain's malt vinegar to America's ketchup to Belgium's mayonnaise.

The origins of the chip are lost in time. Both France and Belgium lay claim to being the country which first came up with the concept of frites. In French potato lore, legend has it that frites were sold on Pont Neuf in Paris by street vendors during the eighteenth century. The Belgians claim that chips come originally from the province of Namur in the south of Belgium. In popular American history, Thomas Jefferson, having been US Minister to France between 1785–89 and who employed a French chef while at the White House as President, is usually credited with introducing chips to America. *The Virginia Housewife*, an American cookbook by Mary Randolph published in 1824, contains a recipe for frying sliced potatoes, either sliced 'a quarter of inch thick' or cut 'in shavings', dried with a cloth and fried in hot lard or dripping 'till they are crisp'. In Britain the first written mention of chips is by the Victorian writer Charles Dickens in his 1859 novel *The Tale of Two Cities*, where he writes of 'husky chips of potatoes, fried with some reluctant drops of oil'. The idea that frying raw potatoes is a French way of cooking is apparent in *Mrs Beeton's 1861 Book*

of *Household Management* where she gives a recipe for 'Fried Potatoes (French Fashion)' which sees thinly sliced potatoes fried in butter or dripping until cooked a 'nice brown'.

Today, it is hard to imagine a world without chips. The success of American-inspired fast food chain restaurants has seen a rise in consumption around the world and they are a staple menu item of major players such as McDonalds, Burger King and KFC. Reportedly, around 7% of all the potatoes grown in the US are turned into French fries by McDonalds, who sell over a third of all the fries sold in the States.

People feel strongly about their chips, returning to establishments that make the sort of chips they enjoy, whether British fish and chip shops or Belgian friteries. When it comes to how to cook them, there is much scope for geekery. To begin with, there is the question of potato variety. Next, comes the question of whether to peel or not to peel the potatoes, Then, the issue of whether to cut the potatoes very thin, thin or thick and chunky. When it comes to frying,

there is a choice of cooking mediums including animal fats like beef dripping or lard and vegetable or sunflower oil. Traditionally, recipes saw chips cooked twice; fried once at a lower temperature to soften the potato without colouring them, then a second time at a higher temperature to crisp up their exterior and give them the desired rich golden hue.

During the 1990s, however, the renowned British chef Heston Blumenthal embarked upon an obsessive quest for the 'perfect chip' and spent several months experimenting with cooking techniques. His resulting three-stage cooking method involves the potatoes first simmered in water to soften them, then frozen to dry them out thoroughly, deep-fried until a light crust forms, frozen again, then deep-fried once again at a higher temperature. This process is undertaken to ensure a chip which has, in Blumenthal's words, 'a glass-like crust and a soft, fluffy centre'. So influential is Blumenthal in the culinary world that the phrase 'triple-cooked chips' now crops up frequently on restaurant menus.

# HASH BROWNS

With their delicate, lacy texture and the contrast between crisp edges and yielding, tender centres, hash browns are a treat! Serve them for a leisurely weekend brunch, with slices of roast ham or grilled/broiled bacon and roasted tomatoes.

600 g/21 oz. potatoes, peeled
salt and freshly ground black pepper
clarified butter or sunflower oil, for shallow-frying
freshly chopped parsley, to garnish

MAKES 12

Grate the potatoes coarsely and place in a large bowl of cold water for 10 minutes; drain.

Wrap the grated potato in a clean kitchen towel and squeeze out the excess moisture. Season the grated potato with salt and freshly ground black pepper, mixing well.

Add enough clarified butter or oil to form a thin layer in a large frying pan/skillet and heat through.

Fry the hash browns in batches. Place four small handfuls of the potato mixture in the frying pan/skillet, spacing them well apart. Use a spatula to press each mound of grated potato down to flatten it out. Fry them until golden brown underneath, then carefully turn over and fry for a few more minutes on the other side. Remove and keep warm. Repeat the process with the remaining grated potato, making 12 hash browns in all. Garnish with parsley and serve with your choice of ham, tomatoes or homemade baked beans.

# POTATO, APPLE AND ONION HASH

The sweetness of the apple together with the subtle nuttiness of the potato and savoury onion makes this simple hash very tasty indeed. Serve it for breakfast or brunch accompanied by bacon or sausages.

**500 g/17½ oz. waxy potatoes, peeled**
**1 tablespoon olive oil**
**1 onion, sliced**
**15 g/1 tablespoon butter**
**1 red-skinned apple, cored and thinly sliced**
**salt and freshly ground black pepper**
**freshly chopped parsley, to garnish**

SERVES 4

Cook the potatoes in boiling, salted water until tender; drain and cut into chunks.

Heat the olive oil in a large frying pan/skillet. Add the onion and fry for 3 minutes, stirring now and then, until softened.

Add the potato chunks and fry, stirring often, for around 5 minutes, until lightly browned. Make a space in the frying pan/skillet and add the butter. Once the butter has melted, add the apple, mixing it with the butter.

Fry the mixture for 5 minutes, stirring often, until the apple is lightly browned. Season with freshly ground black pepper, garnish with parsley and serve at once.

# HOMEMADE POTATO GNOCCHI WITH PIQUANT TOMATO SAUCE

Making your own potato gnocchi from scratch is a satisfying process. Here, the little potato dumplings are served with a gutsy tomato sauce – a tasty combination.

900 g/2 lbs. floury
   potatoes
1 teaspoon salt
100 g/³⁄₄ cup plain/
   all-purpose flour
1 egg, beaten

PIQUANT
TOMATO SAUCE
1 tablespoon olive oil
1 onion, finely chopped
1 bay leaf
1 garlic clove, chopped
1 red (bell) pepper,
   deseeded and
   chopped
splash of dry white wine
1 x 400-g/14-oz. can
   chopped tomatoes
1 teaspoon dried
   Aleppo chilli/hot red
   pepper flakes
salt and freshly ground
   black pepper
grated Parmesan
   cheese, to serve

SERVES 4

Boil the potatoes in their skins until tender; drain. Peel the potatoes while they are still hot and mash them thoroughly with the salt. Mix in the flour and egg and work the mixture to form a soft, slightly sticky dough. Chill the potato dough in the fridge for 30 minutes.

Meanwhile, make the Piquant Tomato Sauce. Heat the olive oil in a frying pan/skillet. Add the onion and bay leaf and fry gently for 2 minutes until the onion is softened. Add the garlic and red (bell) pepper and fry for a further 2 minutes.

Add in the white wine and cook, stirring, for 2 minutes. Add in the tomatoes and season with salt, freshly ground black pepper and the chilli/hot red pepper flakes. Cook for 10 minutes, stirring now and then, until slightly reduced, then remove from the direct heat.

Make the gnocchi by rolling out the chilled dough into 2-cm/³⁄₄-inch thick long rolls. Cut the rolls into 2-cm/³⁄₄-inch pieces. Press each piece against a fork so as to form ridges in each small dumpling.

Gently reheat the Piquant Tomato Sauce. Bring a large pan of water to the boil. Cook the gnocchi in two batches. Add each batch to the boiling water and cook until they float to the surface. Remove with a slotted spoon and keep warm.

Serve the freshly boiled gnocchi with the Piquant Tomato Sauce and grated Parmesan cheese.

# HASSELBACK POTATOES WITH PARMA HAM

Adding pieces of Parma ham/prosciutto to hasselback potatoes makes them even more of a treat! The crispy ham contrasts very nicely with the tender potato, adding a savoury flavour as well as texture. Serve this as a side dish with roast chicken or turkey.

**12 even-sized, small waxy potatoes**
**4 tablespoons olive oil**
**4 slices of Parma ham/ prosciutto, cut into 2.5-cm/1-inch strips**
**salt and freshly ground black pepper**

SERVES 4

Preheat the oven to 200°C (400°F) Gas 6.

Cut slices 3 mm/⅛ inch apart in each of the potatoes, carefully cutting just three-quarters of the way down, so that the slices remain attached to the base of the potato.

Season the potatoes with salt and freshly ground black pepper. Place in a roasting pan and brush thoroughly with the olive oil. Insert a few pieces of Parma ham/prosciutto between the potato slices for each potato.

Roast the potatoes in the preheated oven for 50 minutes–1 hour, until they are cooked through and the edges are lightly browned. Serve at once.

# KALE BUBBLE AND SQUEAK

Adding cooked greens, such as cabbage, Brussels sprouts or kale and fried onion to mashed potato, then frying the mixture is a simple yet effective way of adding texture and flavour. Serve it with crispy bacon, fried eggs and mushrooms for a splendid breakfast or brunch.

600 g/21 oz. potatoes, peeled and chopped
15 g/1 tablespoon butter
splash of milk
freshly grated nutmeg
300 g/10½ oz. kale
2 tablespoons vegetable or sunflower oil
1 onion, finely chopped
salt and freshly ground black pepper

SERVES 4

Cook the potatoes in boiling, salted water until tender. Drain and mash with the butter and milk, seasoning with freshly grated nutmeg and freshly ground black pepper.

Tear the kale leaves from their tough stalks. Cook the kale leaves in a separate pan of boiling water until just tender; drain, squeeze dry and chop.

Heat 1 tablespoon of the oil in a large frying pan/skillet. Add in the onion and fry gently for 5 minutes, stirring often, until softened and lightly browned. Mix the fried onion and kale into the mashed potato.

Heat the remaining oil in the same frying pan/skillet. Add the potato mixture into the pan, flattening it to form an even layer. Fry it over a medium heat, turning occasionally, until browned on both sides. Serve at once.

# STUFFED BAKED POTATOES

Stuffing baked potatoes is a great way to make them into a complete meal. Simply choose and prepare one of the suggested fillings (each one fills four potatoes) and follow the simple method below.

4 baking potatoes, approx. 250 g/9 oz. each

SPINACH AND FETA
250 g/9 oz. spinach
150 g/1 generous cup feta, crumbled
1 teaspoon butter
freshly grated nutmeg
freshly ground black pepper

CHORIZO
1 tablespoon olive oil
½ onion, finely chopped
3 cooking chorizo sausages
freshly ground black pepper

TUNA CAPER
200 g/7 oz. canned tuna in olive oil (drained weight)
1 tablespoon mayonnaise
2 teaspoons capers chopped
1 tablespoon finely chopped chives
freshly ground black pepper

SERVES 4

Preheat the oven to 200°C (400°F) Gas 6.

Pass a skewer through each potato to help it cook evenly. Place them on a baking sheet and bake in the preheated oven for 1 hour until tender. Remove from the oven.

With a sharp knife, cut a narrow slice from the top of each baked potato. Using a teaspoon, carefully scoop out the cooked flesh from the centre of each potato, forming a shell. Mix the potato flesh with the filling of your choice, then fill the potato shells with the mixture. Return to the oven and bake for a further 15 minutes until heated through. Serve at once.

For the spinach and feta filling, rinse the spinach and cook it in a covered pan for 5–8 minutes until wilted. Drain, squeeze dry and chop. Mix together the spinach, feta and butter, seasoning with freshly grated nutmeg and freshly ground black pepper.

For the chorizo filling, heat the olive oil in a frying pan/skillet, add in the onion and fry gently for 5 minutes until softened. Slice open the chorizo sausages, crumble the chorizo into the pan and fry gently for a further 5 minutes. Season with freshly ground black pepper.

For the tuna caper filling, mash together the tuna with the mayonnaise. Mix in the capers and chives and season with freshly ground black pepper.

# LANCASHIRE HOTPOT

A much-loved regional classic of British cuisine, this hearty dish makes an excellent Sunday lunch. The slow-cooked combination of succulent lamb meat and soft, stock-soaked potatoes is truly tasty.

2 tablespoons lard or
goose fat or vegetable
or sunflower oil
8 thick-cut lamb chops
2 turnips, peeled and
chopped into chunks
2 carrots, peeled,
halved lengthways and
cut into 2.5-cm/
1-inch pieces
2 leeks, washed and
thinly sliced
1 tablespoon freshly
chopped parsley, plus
extra to garnish
450 g/15¾ oz.
potatoes, peeled and
very thinly sliced
600 ml/2½ cups lamb,
beef or chicken stock
25 g/1½ tablespoons
butter, melted
salt and freshly ground
black pepper

SERVES 4

Preheat the oven to 200°C (400°F) Gas 6.

Heat the lard, goose fat or oil in a large frying pan/skillet. Fry the lamb chops until lightly browned on both sides and then season with salt and freshly ground black pepper. Remove from the heat.

Layer the ingredients in a heavy-based casserole dish, seasoning the layers with salt and freshly ground black pepper as you do so, as follows. First, place half the turnips, carrots and leeks in the bottom of the dish. Top with the lamp chops, sprinkling them with the parsley. Layer with the remaining turnips, carrots and leeks. Layer the potato slices over the vegetables, overlapping the slices.

Pour the stock into the casserole and, on the hob/stovetop, bring to the boil.

Brush the potato topping with the melted butter. Cover the casserole and bake in the preheated oven for 1¾ hours. Uncover the casserole and bake for a further 15 minutes until the potatoes are golden. Garnish with parsley and serve.

# DANISH-STYLE GLAZED POTATOES

Caramelized potatoes are a classic of Danish cuisine. These sweet,
buttery potatoes are an excellent accompaniment to roast pork,
a joint of ham or a roast goose.

**800 g/28 oz. small,
  even-sized waxy
  potatoes**
**50 g/¼ cup sugar**
**50 g/3½ tablespoons
  butter, diced**
**salt and freshly ground
  black pepper**
**freshly chopped chives
  or parsley, to garnish**

SERVES 4

Boil the potatoes in salted water until tender. Drain, cool and peel.

Sprinkle the sugar in a fine, even layer in a large, heavy-based frying
pan/skillet. Heat the pan over a medium heat until the sugar melts
and caramelizes. Once it turns a light golden brown, add in the butter
and mix in, taking care as the mixture will hiss and splutter.

Add in the peeled potatoes, stirring to coat them in the buttery
caramel. Cook, stirring, for 5 minutes. Season with freshly ground
black pepper. Garnish with chopped chives or parsley and serve
at once.

# PARSLEY POTATO PANCAKES WITH APPLE SAUCE

With their crisp exterior and soft interior, these potato pancakes are a pleasure to eat. The combination of freshly fried pancakes, served warm from the pan, sweet apple sauce and cooling soured/sour cream is a classic one for good reason.

600 g/21 oz. potatoes
1 small onion, finely chopped
115 g/³⁄₄ cup plus 2 tablespoons plain/all-purpose flour
2 eggs, beaten
4 tablespoons freshly chopped parsley
15 g/1 tablespoon butter
salt and freshly ground black pepper
vegetable or sunflower oil, for frying
soured/sour cream, to serve

APPLE SAUCE
700 g/24½ oz. cooking or dessert/eating apples, peeled, quartered, cored and finely chopped
1 cinnamon stick
freshly squeezed juice of ½ lemon
3 tablespoons water
sugar, to taste

MAKES 12

First, make the apple sauce. Place the apples, cinnamon stick, lemon juice and water in a small, heavy-based saucepan. Bring to the boil, cover and cook gently for 5–8 minutes until the apples have softened. Add in sugar to taste and mix well with a wooden spoon to form a soft, thick sauce. Set aside to cool to room temperature.

Peel and coarsely grate the potatoes. Wrap in a clean kitchen towel and squeeze out the excess moisture. Mix together the grated potato, onion, flour and eggs and season with salt and freshly ground black pepper.

Pour enough oil into a large frying pan/skillet so that it forms a shallow layer across the pan. Heat the oil and, when hot, add in the butter, which should sizzle as it hits the pan.

Place four separate tablespoons of the potato mixture in the frying pan/skillet, spaced well apart. Flatten each portion with a spatula to form a rough circle around 5 mm/¼ inch thick. Fry for 2–3 minutes until golden brown underneath, then turn each potato pancake over, pressing down into the hot fat, and fry for a further 2–3 minutes until the other side is golden brown. Remove from the pan, drain on paper towels and keep warm.

Repeat the process with the remaining potato mixture, making 12 pancakes in all. Serve at once with the apple sauce and soured/sour cream and chopped chives (optional).

# POTATO, CHEESE AND CHIVE PIEROGI

There is something very appealing about dumplings – and they taste all the better when you've made them yourself! Pierogi is a much-loved Polish dish – here I've added chives to a classic potato and cheese filling, which gives them a little allium lift!

350 g/2⅔ cups plain/
  all-purpose flour, plus
  extra for dusting
1 teaspoon salt
1 egg, beaten
1 tablespoon vegetable
  or sunflower oil
250 ml/1 cup plus
  1 tablespoon warm
  water

POTATO FILLING
225 g/8 oz. floury
  potatoes, peeled and
  chopped
500 g/17½ oz. cottage
  cheese
20 g/¾ oz. chives,
  finely chopped
freshly grated nutmeg
salt and freshly ground
  pepper

TO SERVE
25 g/1½ tablespoons
  butter, for frying
2–3 tablespoons
  soured/sour cream
paprika, for sprinkling

8-cm/3¼-inch circular
  cutter

MAKES APPROX.
30 PIEROGI

First, make the dough. Sift the flour into a bowl and stir in the salt. Make a well in the centre and add in the egg and oil. Using your fingers, mix the flour with the egg and oil and gradually add and work in the warm water until the mixture comes together to form a soft, sticky dough.

Place the dough on a floured surface and knead well for around 8–10 minutes until smooth and supple. Cover the dough with a clean kitchen towel and chill in the fridge for 1 hour or overnight.

Meanwhile, for the filling, cook the potatoes in boiling, salted water until tender; drain and mash. Set aside to cool. Just before you begin rolling out the dough, mix together the mashed potato, cottage cheese and chives (reserving a tablespoon for garnish). Season with freshly grated nutmeg, salt and freshly ground black pepper.

Thinly roll out the dough on a well floured surface to a thickness of around 3 mm/⅛ inch. Using the circular cutter, cut out rounds from it. To make each pierogi, place a heaped teaspoon of the filling mixture on one half of a dough circle and fold over the dough, pressing and pinching together to seal it well. Place each pierogi spaced well apart (so as not to stick together) on a floured surface.

Bring a large pot of salted water to the boil and cook the pierogi in batches. Gently add in a few pierogi at a time, so as not to overcrowd the pan, and cook for around 2–3 minutes until they float to the surface. Carefully remove them with a slotted spoon and set aside. Repeat the process until all the pierogi have been cooked.

Melt the butter in a large frying pan/skillet. Add in the pierogi and fry for a few minutes on each side until lightly golden brown. Serve the fried pierogi at once, with soured/sour cream, and garnish with paprika, freshly ground black pepper and the reserved chopped chives.

# TRIPLE-COOKED CHIPS

There is something truly irresistible about a good chip! This recipe produces golden brown chips/fries, which are crisp on the outside and tender inside – a tempting combination. Serve them with tasty grilled/broiled steak for a treat of a meal.

**800 g/28 oz. chipping potatoes, such as Christa (Germany) Maris Piper (UK), Idaho (USA)**
**vegetable or sunflower oil, for deep-frying**
**salt**
**mayonnaise, to serve**

*deep fat fryer*

SERVES 4

Peel the potatoes and cut them into 1-cm/½-inch-thick fingers. Rinse the chips/fries 2–3 times in cold water to wash out excess starch.

Place the chips/fries in a pan, cover with cold, salted water. Bring to the boil, then reduce the heat and simmer for 5 minutes; drain. Cover the par-boiled chips/fries with cold water to cool them, drain and chill in the fridge for 30 minutes to firm them up.

Heat enough oil for deep-frying in a deep-fat fryer or a deep pan to a temperature of 130°C (250°F). Add in the chilled chips/fries, cooking in batches so as not to overcrowd the pan, and fry each batch for 5 minutes. They should remain pale and not take on any colour. Remove with a slotted spoon, drain on paper towels and allow to cool.

Heat the same oil for deep-frying in the deep-fat fryer or a deep pan to a temperature of 180°C (350°F). Add in the cooled chips/fries, frying them in batches so as not to overcrowd the pan, until golden brown and crisp, around 3–5 minutes. Remove with a slotted spoon, drain on paper towels, season with salt and serve at once with mayonnaise on the side.

# COD, SWEETCORN AND PRAWN CHOWDER

A tasty version of a classic New England soup. The soft potato and the delicate-textured cod and prawns/shrimp make it at once gentle and comforting. Serve it for lunch or dinner.

2 bacon rashers/ slices, cut into thin strips

50 g/3½ tablespoons butter

1 onion, sliced

1 celery stalk, thinly sliced

1 heaped tablespoon flour

500 ml/2 cups plus 2 tablespoons full-fat milk

500 ml/2 cups plus 2 tablespoons fish stock

400 g/14 oz. floury potatoes, peeled and chopped into small dice

freshly grated nutmeg

500 g/17½ oz. cod or other white fish fillets, skinned and cut into 2.5-cm/ 1-inch cubes

200 g/1½ cups frozen sweetcorn kernels

200 g/1½ cups cooked peeled prawns/shrimp

2 tablespoons freshly chopped parsley

salt and freshly ground black pepper

SERVES 4-6

In a large, heavy-based saucepan, fry the bacon, stirring, for 2 minutes. Add in the butter and once it foams, add in the onion and celery. Fry gently for 2–3 minutes until softened. Mix in the flour, stirring in well, and fry briefly.

Gradually stir in first the milk, then the fish stock. Stirring, bring to the boil and cook until thickened.

Add in the diced potatoes and simmer for 5–10 minutes until tender. Season with freshly grated nutmeg, salt and freshly ground black pepper.

Bring to the boil, add in the cod or other white fish and sweetcorn and simmer for 3–5 minutes until the fish is cooked. Add in the prawns/shrimp and simmer for 2 minutes. Stir in the parsley and serve.

# JANSSON'S TEMPTATION

This classic Swedish gratin is comfort food in potato form! The cured, spiced Swedish sprats, which are a traditional element, add a distinctive, aromatic and salty-sweet flavour to the dish. The resulting dish has a sticky, creamy richness to it, which makes it very beguiling.

50 g/3½ tablespoons
  butter
2 large onions, thinly
  sliced
900 g/2 lbs. waxy
  potatoes
1 x 125-g/4½-oz. can
  Swedish sprat fillets or
  pickled herrings in a
  traditional brine
150 ml/generous
  ¼ cup double/heavy
  cream
150 ml/scant ⅔ cup
  full-fat milk
salt

SERVES 6–8

Preheat the oven to 220°C (425°F) Gas 7.

Use 25 g/1½ tablespoons of the butter to generously grease an ovenproof dish.

Fry the onions gently in the remaining butter in a frying pan/skillet, stirring often, for 10 minutes, until softened. Remove from the heat.

Peel the potatoes and cut them into short, thin, matchstick pieces. Layer a quarter of the potato pieces in the bottom of the greased dish, seasoning lightly with salt. Top with a third of the fried onions and a third of the sprat fillets or pickled herrings (being sure to reserve their brine). Repeat the process, finishing with a layer of potato pieces.

Pour the reserved sprat or pickled herring brine over the mixture. Mix together the cream and milk and pour half of it over the mixture (reserve the rest).

Bake in the preheated oven for 30 minutes, then pour over the remaining cream mixture. Return to the oven to bake for a further 30 minutes, until the potatoes are cooked and the top of the dish is lightly browned. Serve at once.

# POTATO CHEESE PIE

A homely recipe, which all the family will enjoy. The crisp, buttery pastry contrasts nicely with the soft, cheesy potato filling.

**PASTRY**
225 g/1¾ cups plain/ all-purpose flour
pinch of salt
125 g/½ cup plus 1 tablespoon butter

**FILLING**
400 g/14 oz. potatoes, peeled and cut into chunks
2 onions, quartered and thinly sliced
1 tablespoon vegetable or sunflower oil
100 g/1 cup plus 2 tablespoons grated Cheddar cheese
freshly grated nutmeg
25 g/1½ tablespoons butter
2 tablespoons freshly chopped parsley
milk, for brushing
salt and freshly ground black pepper

*1 deep, loose-based 20-cm/8-inch fluted tart pan, greased*

SERVES

First, make the pastry. Mix together the flour and salt, rub in the butter with your fingertips until absorbed, then mix in 2–3 tablespoons of cold water so that the mixture comes together to form a dough. Wrap and chill in the fridge for 30 minutes.

For the filling, cook the potatoes in boiling, salted water until tender; drain.

Meanwhile, gently fry the onions in the oil over a low heat, stirring often, for 10 minutes, until thoroughly softened.

Mash the cooked potatoes thoroughly with the butter. Season well with freshly grated nutmeg, salt and freshly ground black pepper. Stir in the Cheddar cheese, fried onions and parsley. Set aside to cool.

Preheat the oven to 200°C (400°F) Gas 6.

Roll out two-thirds of the pastry. Use the pastry to line the prepared tart pan. Fill the pastry case with the potato mixture.

Roll out the remaining pastry and cut out a pie lid. Brush the edges of the pie case with milk and top with the pie lid, pressing the edges together to seal well. Brush the pastry lid with milk and cut three slashes in the centre of the pie.

Bake the pie in the preheated oven for 50 minutes until golden brown. Serve hot, warm or at room temperature.

# SPICY
# POTATOES

# CULINARY POTATOES

Where would the cook be without the potato?! A 'wholesome and delicious vegetable' wrote Isabella Beeton of the tuber in her bestselling Victorian cookbook, *Beeton's Book of Household Management*. She gives detailed recipes for potatoes cooked in a variety of ways: in their jackets, as they are 'always served' in Ireland, *a la Maitre d'Hotel* (boiled, sliced and cooked with parsley, gravy and lemon juice), using 'a German method' (cooked in a brown roux-based sauce) and Potato Snow. With regard to new potatoes, she observes 'Do not have the potatoes dug out long before they are dressed as they are never good when they have been out of the ground some time.' There are also a number of thrifty recipes – including mashed potato cakes baked in the oven rather than fried and potato rissoles, enhanced with minced/ground tongue or ham – demonstrating the vegetable's useful scope for economical housekeeping.

The potato's delicate flavour and starchy texture make it a very versatile ingredient indeed. That unobtrusive taste makes it an excellent accompaniment to full-flavoured main courses: mashed or creamed potato, served alongside rich, slow-cooked stews or new potatoes, boiled in their skins, as a side with grilled/broiled fish or lamb chops. And it's impossible to envision a roast lunch of chicken or rib of beef without its mandatory serving of golden-brown roast potatoes (see page 144)! Similarly, in many dishes the subtle nutty flavour of potatoes is used as a foil to a more assertive sauce, as with Spain's tapas dish patatas bravas which sees fried potatoes served with a chilli-hot piquant sauce or Indonesia's gado-gado salad (see recipe page 31).

One of the reasons why the potato can be used in so many different ways is the range of textures it offers.

It is an aspect of cooking potatoes which is evident in the recipes in this book, where I specify texture when appropriate to the dish. Waxy potatoes, with their more compact texture, are excellent in dishes that require potatoes to hold their texture, classically potato salad, that stalwart of buffets, or a creamy, baked potato gratin. Floury potatoes, with their noticeably light, fluffy texture, work well in dishes such as mash. In countries including Germany, Italy, Peru and Russia, one finds the custom of using mashed potatoes to make a dough from which dumplings, plain or filled, are then made (see recipe for mushroom-filled dumplings on page 64). In soups, potatoes are a useful thickener, adding body to Portugal's famous caldo verde (see page 51) and American seafood chowders (see page 97) and a velvety texture to France's classic Vichyssoise (see page 28).

The potato's capacity to soak up flavour is also appreciated by cooks around the world. In Malaysia and Indonesia, kari ayam is a popular chicken curry which sees both pieces of chicken and chopped potato simmered in a spiced coconut milk gravy. As it cooks, the potato becomes saturated to delicious effect – try the recipe on page 125 and you'll see what I mean! This sponge-like aspect is also used when making potato salads, with boiled, peeled potatoes dressed while still warm with vinegar-based dressings so that the flavour permeates the vegetable.

Another popular way of enhancing potatoes found in cuisines around the world is to mix other ingredients – such as fried onions, chillies, spices and herbs – in with cooked potatoes to make a flavourful potato mixture. Perkedel kentang are Indonesian croquettes, made from spiced mince/ground meat and mashed potato. In South India, large, crisp-textured pancakes called dosai are filled with mashed potatoes flavoured with onion, ginger, garlic

and spices. In Europe, mashed potato dishes such as Ireland's champ (flavoured with spring onion/scallion), or colcannon (with cabbage) or Britain's bubble and squeak (made with Brussels sprouts or cabbage and onion) are much-loved, while in America one finds corned beef hash and red flannel hash, a variant made with beetroot and onion.

Potatoes, of course, lend themselves beautifully to frying, turning golden brown and acquiring a satisfying crispness in the process. Chips or French fries, the best-known example of this, are explored on page 94. There are, however, numerous variations on the fried potato theme, using factors such as deep-frying or shallow-frying, the frying medium, whether the potato is raw or cooked when fried or sliced or mashed to create a range of dishes. France has a rich tradition of fried potato dishes such as sautéed potatoes, soufflé potatoes and potato croquettes. In Jewish cuisine, the festival of Hanukkah is celebrated by eating foods fried in oil, among them latkes made from shredded potatoes.

# PIQUANT POTATO STRAWS

There is something irresistible about these dainty, crisp-textured
potato straws. Serve them as an accompaniment for gin and tonics
for pre-dinner drinks.

**400 g/14 oz. potatoes**
**1 teaspoon hot smoked**
**paprika or pimentón**
**1 teaspoon mild**
**smoked paprika or**
**pimentón**
**1–2 teaspoons salt**
**oil, for deep-frying**

SERVES 8–10 AS A
NIBBLE

Peel the potatoes and cut into short, thin matchstick strips. Rinse
in cold water, then pat dry thoroughly.

Heat enough oil for deep-frying in a deep pan or wok to 180°C/350°F
or until a small piece of bread added to the hot oil browns within
60 seconds.

Fry the potato straws in batches, so as not to overcrowd the pan.
Cook them until they turn golden brown on all sides, remove with
a slotted spoon and drain on paper towels.

Toss the freshly fried potato straws at once with the two types of
paprika or pimentón and the salt, mixing thoroughly. Serve at once.

# CAULIFLOWER POTATO CURRY

This quickly-made, dry vegetable curry is gutsy, piquant and fragrant. Serve it with chapatis or steamed basmati rice for a vegan meal, ideal for a mid-week supper.

300 g/10½ oz. waxy potatoes

1 cauliflower, cut into florets

1½ tablespoons vegetable or sunflower oil

1 onion, finely chopped

2-cm/¾-inch piece of fresh ginger, peeled and finely chopped

1 garlic clove, chopped

1 teaspoon fennel seeds

1 teaspoon mustard seeds

2 teaspoons ground cumin

1 teaspoon ground turmeric

½ teaspoon chilli/chili powder

2 tablespoons tomato purée/paste

150 ml/scant ⅔ cup hot water

1 teaspoon sugar

salt

freshly chopped coriander/cilantro, to garnish

SERVES 4

Cook the potatoes in boiling, salted water until tender; drain and quarter. In a separate pan, par-boil the cauliflower in boiling, salted water for 5 minutes until just tender; drain.

Heat the oil in a large, heavy-based frying pan/skillet over a medium heat. Fry the onion, stirring often, for 5 minutes, until softened. Add in the ginger, garlic, fennel seeds and mustard seeds and fry, stirring, for 2 minutes until fragrant.

Mix the cumin, turmeric and chilli/chili powder with a tablespoon of cold water to make a spice paste. Add in the spice paste to the onion mixture and cook, stirring, for 1 minute. Add in the potato quarters and cauliflower, mixing in well.

Mix the tomato purée/paste into the hot water and add to the potato mixture. Season with salt and add in the sugar. Mix well. Bring to the boil, cover and cook for 5 minutes, stirring now and then. Garnish with coriander/cilantro and serve.

# POTATO SAMOSAS WITH TAMARIND CHUTNEY

With their crisp filo coating and spicy potato filling, these homemade samosas, served with a tangy tamarind chutney, are hard to resist.

2 tablespoons oil

1 onion, finely chopped

2.5-cm/1-inch piece of fresh ginger, peeled and finely chopped

1 tablespoon cumin seeds

500 g/17½ oz. potatoes, peeled, boiled, finely diced

100 g/3½ oz. frozen peas, thawed

100 g/3½ oz. frozen sweetcorn, thawed

2 teaspoons ground coriander

½ teaspoon chilli/chili powder

½ teaspoon ground turmeric

freshly squeezed juice of ½ lemon

½ teaspoon sugar

5 filo sheets (36 x 31 cm/14 x 12 inches)

50 g/3½ tablespoons butter, melted

salt and freshly ground black pepper

TAMARIND CHUTNEY

2 heaped tablespoons tamarind pulp

120 ml/½ cup hot water

8 pitted dates

MAKES 20 SAMOSAS

First, prepare the filling. Heat the oil in a large frying pan/skillet over a medium heat. Add in the onion and fry gently until softened. Add in the ginger and cumin seeds and fry, stirring, for 1–2 minutes until fragrant.

Add in the potatoes, peas and sweetcorn. Sprinkle over the coriander, chilli/chili powder and turmeric, mixing well, and season with salt and freshly ground black pepper. Add in the lemon juice and sugar and mix together. Fry, stirring now and then, for 5 minutes. Set aside to cool.

Preheat the oven to 200°C (400°F) Gas 6.

Slice the filo sheets each into four strips. Cover the filo strips you're not using with a clean kitchen towel, to prevent them from drying out.

Lightly brush a filo strip with melted butter. Place a teaspoon of the potato mixture in one corner of the strip and then fold the pastry diagonally over the filling several times to form a neat triangular filo parcel, brushing the pastry with melted butter as you do so. Brush the exterior of the samosa with melted butter and place on a greased baking sheet. Repeat the process, making 20 samosas in all.

Bake the samosas in the preheated oven for 20 minutes until golden brown.

While they bake, make the tamarind chutney. Soak the tamarind pulp in a small bowl of hot water for 15 minutes to soften, then strain to remove the fibres and seeds from the tamarind paste.

In a food processor, blend together the tamarind paste, measured hot water and the dates until smooth.

Serve the samosas warm or at room temperature with the tamarind chutney on the side.

# POTATO WEDGES WITH ROMESCO SAUCE

Warm potato wedges – with their mild nuttiness – are an excellent foil for tangy, flavourful romesco, a classic Spanish sauce.

600 g/21 oz. even-sized
  potatoes
4 tablespoon extra
  virgin olive oil
salt

ROMESCO SAUCE
300 g/10½ oz.
  tomatoes
4 garlic cloves
75 g/½ cup toasted
  hazelnuts
2 dried red chillies/
  chiles, soaked in
  warm water for
  20 minutes, drained
1–2 tablespoons red
  wine vinegar
freshly chopped parsley
  to serve

SERVES 4

Preheat the oven to 200°C (400°F) Gas 6.

Peel the potatoes, halve each one lengthways and slice each half into four wedges, making eight wedges in all per potato. Toss the wedges with 1 tablespoon of the olive oil and season with salt. Place in a roasting pan and bake in the preheated oven for 40–50 minutes until tender and blotched golden brown.

Meanwhile, for the romesco sauce, place the tomatoes in a separate roasting pan and bake in the preheated oven alongside the potatoes for 30 minutes, until their skins split. Remove from the oven.

Blanch the garlic cloves in a small pan of boiling water for 3 minutes; drain and peel.

To finish the romesco sauce, peel the roast tomatoes. In a food processor, pulse-blend the hazelnuts and soaked chillies/chiles until roughly ground. Add in the tomatoes and garlic and blend to form a soft, textured paste. Stir in the remaining olive oil and add the vinegar to taste. Season with salt. Serve the potato wedges warm from the oven with the romesco sauce on the side.

# INDIAN FIVE-SPICE SAUTÉED POTATOES

An aromatic Indian spice mixture, known as panch phoran, gives a
pleasing fragrance to sautéed potatoes. Serve this as a side dish as
part of an Indian meal, or for a spicy brunch dish.

**500 g/17½ oz.
even-sized waxy
potatoes**
**1 tablespoon oil**
**2 teaspoons panch
phoran spice mixture
or ¾ teaspoon cumin
seeds, ½ teaspoon
fennel seeds,
¼ teaspoon yellow
mustard seeds,
¼ teaspoon nigella
seeds (kalonji) mixed
together**
**1 long dried red chilli/
chile**
**½ onion, finely chopped**
**½ teaspoon paprika**
**2 tablespoons freshly
chopped coriander/
cilantro leaves**
**salt and freshly ground
black pepper**

SERVES 4

Cook the potatoes in boiling, salted water until tender; drain. Peel and
slice into 5-mm/¼-inch thick slices.

Heat the oil in a large frying pan/skillet. Add in the panch phoran
spice mixture or mixed seeds and the dried chilli/chile and fry,
stirring, for just under 1 minute until fragrant.

Add in the potato slices and fry for 5 minutes. Remove and discard
the dried chilli/chile. Add in the chopped onion and stir to mix.

Fry for 10–15 minutes until the potatoes are lightly browned on both
sides. Season with salt and freshly ground black pepper. Sprinkle
with paprika and chopped coriander/cilantro and serve at once.

# TURMERIC POTATO WRAPS

Inspired by India's dosai pancakes, these wraps make a tasty, easy vegetarian meal. Serve with mango chutney for a light lunch or supper.

500 g/17½ oz. floury potatoes, peeled and cut into chunks
2 teaspoons black mustard seeds
2 tablespoons ghee or vegetable or sunflower oil
1 onion, finely chopped
2.5-cm/1-inch piece of fresh ginger, peeled and chopped
2 garlic cloves, chopped
½ teaspoon ground turmeric
1 teaspoon ground cumin
1 teaspoon ground coriander
¼ teaspoon chilli/ chili powder (optional)
½ teaspoon sugar
freshly squeezed juice of ½ lemon
salt and freshly ground black pepper
4 tablespoons freshly chopped coriander/ cilantro leaves (reserving some to garnish)
4 tortilla wraps
mango chutney, to serve

MAKES 4 WRAPS

Cook the potatoes in boiling, salted water until tender; drain and mash.

Heat the mustard seeds in a dry frying pan/ skillet, stirring, for 1 minute. Add in the ghee or oil, heat through and then add in the onion and fry gently for 5 minutes. Add in the ginger and garlic and fry for 1 minute until fragrant. Add in the turmeric, cumin, ground coriander and chilli/ chili powder (if using) and mix well.

Add the spiced onion mixture to the mashed potato, mixing in well. Mix in the sugar, lemon juice and chopped coriander/cilantro. Season with salt and freshly ground black pepper.

Heat each tortilla wrap briefly in a microwave or a hot frying pan/skillet. Place a quarter of the turmeric potato mixture in the centre of a tortilla; fold over the filling. Repeat with the remaining potato mixture and tortillas, garnish with the reserved chopped coriander/cilantro and serve at once with mango chutney.

# KIMCHI POTATO CAKES

These small potato cakes – a piquant riff on classic potato dishes, such as Britain's bubble and squeak or Ireland's colcannon – are very tasty indeed. Serve with fried eggs, and topped with sliced spring onions/scallions for a satisfying breakfast or brunch.

700 g/24½ oz. potatoes, peeled and chopped
2 spring onions/ scallions, finely chopped
25 g/1½ tablespoons butter
150 g/5½ oz. kimchi, finely chopped
salt and freshly ground black pepper
vegetable or sunflower oil, for shallow-frying

SERVES 4

Cook the potatoes in boiling, salted water until tender. As they cook, gently fry the spring onions/scallions in the butter in a frying pan/ skillet until softened but not browned.

Drain the cooked potatoes, add in the fried spring onion/scallions with its butter and mash well. Season with freshly ground black pepper. Mix in the kimchi.

Working with oiled hands, take tablespoons of the mixture and shape into 16 small, even-sized potato cakes.

Pour enough oil into a large frying pan/skillet so that it forms a shallow layer in the pan and heat through over a medium heat. Add in the potato cakes, frying in batches if need be, and cook for a few minutes on each side until browned. Remove, drain on paper towels and serve at once.

# POTATO BEAN QUESADILLAS

With its rich combination of filling ingredients – piquant potatoes and beans, soured/sour cream and cheese – these Mexican-inspired quesadillas make a great vegetarian meal, ideal for a light lunch or supper. Serve with a fresh green side salad made from avocado, crisp lettuce and radishes, dressed with lemon juice and olive oil.

400 g/14 oz. floury
  potatoes, peeled and
  chopped
1 garlic clove, crushed
1 teaspoon chipotle
  chilli/chili paste
1 x 400-g/14-oz. can
  black or kidney beans,
  drained and rinsed
4 x 20-cm/8-inch soft
  tortillas
4 tablespoons soured/
  sour cream
100 g/1 cup grated
  Cheddar cheese
4 cherry tomatoes, each
  sliced into 3
coriander/cilantro
  leaves
salt and freshly ground
  black pepper

SERVES 4

Cook the potatoes in boiling, salted water until tender; drain. Mash the potatoes with the garlic and chipotle paste, mixing well. Season with salt and freshly black ground pepper. Mix in the beans.

Take one of the tortillas and spread half of it with a layer of the potato mixture. Top with 1 tablespoon of soured/sour cream, sprinkle over 25 g/¼ cup grated Cheddar cheese, top with three cherry tomato slices and a sprinkling of coriander/cilantro leaves. Fold the tortilla over the filling. Repeat the process with the remaining tortillas and other ingredients, forming four quesadillas.

Heat a large, heavy-based frying pan/skillet until hot. Dry-fry the quesadillas over medium heat, starting with them folded-side down, turning once, until golden-brown on both sides. Serve at once.

# POTATO CORIANDER PAKORAS

Pakoras are a tasty Indian snack, a popular party nibble to serve with drinks. These small, light fritters offer a delicious contrast between the tasty fragrant batter and the potato filling.

190 g/½ cup chickpea/gram flour
1½ teaspoons salt, plus extra for seasoning
1 teaspoon garam masala
½ teaspoon chilli/chili powder
½ teaspoon ground turmeric
1 teaspoon nigella seeds (kalonji)
300 g/10½ oz. potatoes
1 large onion, finely chopped
1 garlic clove, finely chopped
1 small bunch of coriander/cilantro, finely chopped, plus extra leaves to garnish
freshly squeezed juice of ½ lime
150 ml/¾ cup natural/plain yogurt
vegetable or sunflower oil for deep-frying

MAKES APPROX. 32

First make the batter. Sift the chickpea/gram flour, 1½ teaspoons salt, the garam masala, chilli/chili powder and turmeric into a mixing bowl. Whisk in 200 ml/¾ cup of water to form a thick batter, then stir in the nigella seeds and set aside to rest for 30 minutes.

Peel and finely dice the potatoes. Mix the potatoes, onion, garlic and 4 tablespoons of the chopped coriander/cilantro into the batter.

Make a dipping sauce by mixing the remaining coriander/cilantro and lime juice into the yogurt. Season with salt. Set aside.

Heat enough oil for deep-frying in a deep pan or wok to 180°C/350°F or until a small piece of bread added to the hot oil browns within 60 seconds.

Fry the pakoras in batches. To form the individual pakoras, drop spoonfuls of the potato mixture, spaced apart, into the hot oil. Fry until they turn a rich golden brown on all sides. Remove with a slotted spoon, drain on paper towels and keep warm until serving.

Once all the batter has been used up, serve the pakoras at once accompanied by the yogurt dipping sauce and garnished with coriander/cilantro leaves.

# MALAYSIAN CHICKEN AND POTATO CURRY

This Malaysian chicken curry is a gloriously aromatic affair, given creamy richness by the coconut milk, while the new potatoes soak up the spicy gravy in the nicest possible way. Serve with jasmine or basmati rice for a delicious meal.

2 lemongrass stalks
3 tablespoons oil
2 onions, finely chopped
2 garlic cloves, chopped
2-cm/³/₄-inch piece of ginger, peeled and finely chopped
8 chicken thighs
400 ml/1³/₄ cups canned coconut milk
4 kaffir lime leaves
1 cinnamon stick
8 small new potatoes
salt

CURRY POWDER
1 star anise
1 teaspoon fennel seeds
4 cloves
1 tablespoon ground coriander
2 teaspoons ground cumin
1 teaspoon ground white pepper
2 teaspoons ground cinnamon
1 teaspoon ground turmeric
1 teaspoon chilli/chili powder
½ nutmeg, finely grated

SERVES 4

First, make the curry powder. Using a pestle and mortar or a spice grinder, finely grind the star anise, fennel seeds and cloves. Mix these together with all the other curry powder spices. Set aside.

Peel and discard the tough outer casing of the lemongrass stalks. Finely chop the white bulbous part of the stalks, discarding the remainder.

Heat the oil in a flameproof casserole dish. Add in the onions, garlic, ginger and lemongrass and fry gently, stirring, for 5 minutes until the onions have softened.

Mix the curry powder with 2–3 tablespoons of cold water to form a paste. Add the paste to the onion mixture and fry gently, stirring, for 3 minutes until fragrant.

Add in the chicken thighs and coat in the paste. Add in the coconut milk, 100 ml/⅓ cup of water, a little salt, the kaffir lime leaves and cinnamon stick. Bring to the boil, reduce the heat, cover and cook for 30 minutes. Add in the new potatoes and cook, covered, for a further 30 minutes until the chicken is cooked through and the potatoes are tender. Serve.

# ZAHTAR ROAST POTATOES

Zahtar – a mixture of wild thyme, sumac, sesame seeds and salt –
is a popular spice mixture used in the Middle East. It is usually
eaten with pitta bread and oil or used to top flatbreads. My simple,
unorthodox recipe uses zahtar as a flavouring for potatoes. The
results are delightfully aromatic roast potatoes, which make an
excellent accompaniment to slow-roast lamb or roast chicken.

500 g/17½ oz. small,
  even-sized waxy
  potatoes
1 tablespoon olive oil
1 tablespoon zahtar
sea salt flakes

SERVES 4

Preheat the oven to 200°C (400°F) Gas 6.

Toss the potatoes with the olive oil, coating evenly. Add the zahtar
and season with a pinch or so of salt, mixing together well.

Place the potatoes in a roasting pan and roast in the preheated
oven for 40–50 minutes until tender, turning now and then to
ensure even cooking.

Sprinkle a pinch of sea salt flakes over them
and serve at once, hot from the oven.

# POTATO, SWEET POTATO AND CARROT DHAL

Adding root vegetables to a classic Indian dhal is an effective way of making it into a substantial meal. The texture of the tender root vegetables contrasts nicely with the thick lentil purée. Serve this with steamed basmati rice or chapatis.

1 tablespoon vegetable or sunflower oil

1 onion, finely chopped

3 garlic cloves, chopped

2.5-cm/1-inch piece of fresh ginger, peeled and finely chopped

1 teaspoon mustard seeds

8 curry leaves

2 teaspoons ground cumin

1 teaspoon ground turmeric

250 g/1½ cups dried split red lentils

2 tomatoes, chopped

1 teaspoon sugar

4 waxy potatoes, quartered

1 sweet potato/yam, peeled and chopped into 2.5 cm/1 inch cubes, tossed with a squeeze of lemon juice to prevent them from discolouring

1 carrot, peeled, halved lengthways, cut into 2.5 cm/ 1 inch pieces

1 tablespoon ghee

a handful of fresh coriander/cilantro leaves

salt

SERVES 4

Heat the oil in a heavy-based saucepan. Add the onion and fry, stirring often, for 5 minutes until softened and lightly browned. Add in two cloves of chopped garlic, the ginger, mustard seeds, curry leaves, cumin and turmeric and fry, stirring, for 1 minute.

Add in the lentils, tomatoes, 900 ml/4 cups of water, a little salt and the sugar. Bring to the boil, reduce the heat and cook, partly covered, for 20 minutes, stirring now and then, until the lentils have softened.

Add in the potatoes, sweet potato/yam and carrot and bring back to the boil. Cover the pan, reduce the heat and simmer for 30 minutes, stirring now and then, until the root vegetables are tender. Taste and season with more salt if needed.

Heat the ghee in a small frying pan/skillet. Add in the remaining garlic and fry, stirring, until golden brown. Pour the fried garlic together with the hot ghee at once over the lentil mixture and stir in. Add the coriander/cilantro leaves and stir in. Serve at once.

# POTATO CHAAT MASALA

Based on a popular Indian street food, this is a lively potato and chickpea dish, offering an appealing mixture of flavours and textures. Serve it as a first course for an Indian meal, or enjoy as a light lunch with flatbreads or poppadoms on the side.

300 g/10½ oz. waxy potatoes, peeled
juice of 1 lime or ½ lemon
150 g/5½ oz. canned chickpeas, drained, rinsed and patted dry
½ small onion, finely chopped
1 mild green chilli/chile, deseeded and thinly sliced
2 handfuls of coriander/cilantro leaves, roughly chopped
3 tablespoons natural/plain yogurt
2 tablespoons Tamarind Chutney (see page 110) or 1 tablespoon tamarind paste
salt
lime wedges, to serve

CHAAT MASALA
2 teaspoons ground cumin
1 teaspoon amchoor (dried mango powder)
½ teaspoon chilli/chili powder
½ teaspoon freshly ground black pepper
seeds from 1 cardamom pod, finely ground
½ teaspoon salt
½ teaspoon sugar

SERVES 4

Cook the potatoes in boiling, salted water until tender; drain and dice.

Meanwhile, mix together all the chaat masala ingredients. While the potatoes are still warm, toss them with the lime or lemon juice and chaat masala, mixing well.

Add the chickpeas, onion, chilli/chile and coriander/cilantro to the potatoes and mix well. Cover and set aside at room temperature for 30 minutes to allow the flavours to develop.

Top first with the yogurt, then the Tamarind Chutney or tamarind paste. Serve at once with wedges of lime and flatbreads or poppadoms.

LUXURIOUS
POTATOES

# MEET THE POTATO FARMERS

**The Jersey Royal farmers, Jersey, British Isles**
The distinctive kidney-shaped Jersey Royal potato, with its thin skin, delicate, fresh flavour and creamy texture, was first planted on the island of Jersey in the Channel Islands in 1878 by farmer Hugh de la Haye. Historically, these potatoes were the UK's first new season potato of the year.

Jersey Royals come into season in March and are then harvested through to June, with May seeing the bulk of the crop. The labour-intensive cycle of cultivating Jersey Royals, defined by a Protected Designation of Origin, begins each autumn. First, every Jersey Royal seed potato is graded by hand into different sizes and the shoot which has formed is knocked off in order to encourage more new shoots to grow. The size of the potato determines in which fields they will be planted, with the larger ones planted on fields more prone to frost. Steep, south-facing, sloping fields, which receive a lot of sunlight, are planted by hand with potatoes, each one with the shoots pointing upwards, covered with fleece in the event of harsh frosts. It is these which are the first to be harvested, dug up by hand in March and April. Seaweed, thrown onto the beaches, is a traditional fertiliser for some of the fields, especially on the sandy-soiled west of the island.

The growing of these highly-prized potatoes is now engrained into island culture, with over half the arable land on Jersey used for cultivating them and farmers proud of maintaining this agricultural heritage. It is not only the island's farmers which grow them. Each year sees all the primary schools in Jersey take part in Jersey Royal growing competitions. So, too, do the island's Parish constables and the Women's Institute groups, with much friendly rivalry as to who can grow the best.

Fleece-covered Jersey Royals

**Carroll's Heritage Potatoes, Tiptoe Farm, Northumberland, Britain** Shetland Black, Colleen, Mr Little's Yetholm Gypsy – these intriguingly-named, little-known cultvars are among the 20 or so heritage potato varieties grown by Lucy and Anthony Carroll on Tiptoe Farm in rural Northumberland, Britain. The couple were working as farmers growing ordinary potato varieties for a packer, while growing interesting heritage potatoes in their garden for themselves. "We had a lightbulb moment," explains Lucy. "We thought, these heritage potatoes are amazing – what would people think of them?" In 2000, the Carrolls planted a trial acre of heritage potato varieties and took them to their local farmers' market in Berwick upon Tweed to see what the people thought. "The response was phenomenal," remembers Lucy happily.

Lucy explains that these older varieties don't yield as well as modern varieties and so have fallen out of favour commercially. "Growing them is an expensive business," she says laughing ruefully, "as they're low yielding and susceptible to disease, but to us the advantages outweigh the disadvantages." The Carrolls have worked hard to build up a network of customers, with chefs in Britain a key part of their market. "We have a reputation now and what we provide is a very personal service to chefs. Whereas before we came along they ordered just one potato for lots, they now appreciate having the right potato for the right job. A pink fir apple potato is fantastic in salads, while our Mayan Golds are amazing roasted!"

**The Little Organic Farm, Petaluna, Marin County, California, USA**
Chez Panisse, Coi, The French Laundry, Manresa, Zuni . . .the roll-call of restaurants which Californian farmer David Little supplies with organic potatoes is truly an impressive one; these are legendary West Coast establishments, known around the world for the quality of the food they offer. "A lot of famous chefs love these potatoes," says David with quiet satisfaction. "They're grown with no irrigation. It gives low yields but we get an intense flavour."

Dry-farming, explains David, is a traditional method of farming, brought to California by European immigrants during the nineteenth century. "They settled here and there was very little water, so they dry-farmed crops and saved their water for their livestock." As agriculture intensified during the twentieth century, however, dry-farming, with its low yields fell out of favour. "When I started in 1995, I was the only one doing it and I'm still the only one – what does that tell you?!" In growing potatoes, Little is also maintaining another local tradition. "I used to hang out at the tavern talking to the old-timers there. The hills here used to be covered with potatoes until the war." David grows a number of potatoes suitable for various cooking methods, with Carola, from Germany, and another variety called French among his favourites.

# PERSIAN-STYLE SAFFRON RICE WITH POTATOES

Fragrant with spices, this textured pilaff made from long-grained basmati is an elegant rice dish, perfect for entertaining. Serve with marinated roast lamb, barbecued chicken kebabs/kabobs or a roast aubergine/eggplant salad for a Middle Eastern-inspired feast.

250 g/1⅓ cups
  basmati rice
1 teaspoon saffron
  threads, finely ground,
  or 1 teaspoon saffron
  powder
2 tablespoons hot water
4 tablespoons sunflower
  or vegetable oil
1 onion, finely chopped
200 g/7 oz. waxy
  potatoes, peeled and
  diced into 1-cm/
  ½-inch cubes
2 tablespoons dried
  barberries or currants
1 tablespoon pine nuts
15 g/1 tablespoon
  butter
1 teaspoon ground
  cinnamon
salt

SERVES 6

Rinse the basmati rice 2–3 times to wash out excess starch. Cover in cold water and set aside to soak for 45 minutes.

Mix the ground saffron with the hot water and set aside to infuse.

Heat the oil in a heavy-based saucepan. Add in the onion and fry gently over a low heat, stirring now and then, for 5 minutes until softened. Add in the potato cubes, increase the heat to medium and fry, stirring often, for 8 minutes, until lightly browned. Add in the barberries or currents and pine nuts and fry, stirring, for 2 minutes.

Add in the butter. Once it has melted, add in the ground cinnamon, mixing well.

Drain the soaked rice and add to the pan, mixing well. Add 300 ml/1¼ cups of water, saffron liquid and the salt. Bring to the boil. Cover, reduce the heat and cook over a very low heat for 15 minutes until the water has been absorbed and the rice is tender. Serve at once.

# ROSEMARY GARLIC POTATOES

Very simple indeed to make, these roast potatoes with their Mediterranean flavours are a pleasure to eat! Serve them as a side-dish with a succulent, slow-cooked lamb stew, tasty roast chicken or grilled sea bass fillets.

1 kg/35 oz. waxy
  potatoes
2 tablespoons olive oil
salt
1 garlic bulb, broken up
  into individual garlic
  cloves
8 sprigs of rosemary,
  cut into 2.5-cm/
  1-inch pieces

SERVES 6

Preheat the oven to 220°C (425°F) Gas 7.

Peel the potatoes and, depending on their size, cut them into quarters or halves; you want them to be evenly sized in order to ensure even cooking.

Bring a large pan of salted water to the boil. Add in the potatoes and par-boil for 10 minutes. Drain them thoroughly, return to the pan and shake them in the pan to roughen their surfaces.

Add the olive oil to a roasting pan, place in the oven and heat through until the oil becomes very hot.

Add the potato chunks to the hot olive oil, tossing and turning them so as to coat them evenly in it, and season with salt. Add in the garlic cloves and rosemary, mixing well. Roast in the preheated oven for around 40–45 minutes until the potatoes are golden brown all over, turning now and then to ensure even browning. Serve at once.

# SEAFOOD NEW POTATO SALAD

This pretty dish is a gloriously indulgent take on potato salad. The smooth, sweet nuttiness of the new potatoes is the perfect showcase for the seafood flavours of crab and prawns/shrimp, with the asparagus and quail's eggs adding additional colour, flavour and texture.

100 g/3½ oz.
asparagus
500 g/17½ oz. waxy
potatoes, peeled,
or Jersey Royals,
washed
3 heaped tablespoons
mayonnaise
1 tablespoon crème
fraîche
1 teaspoon extra virgin
olive oil
4 tablespoons freshly
chopped tarragon
leaves
1 small dressed crab
100 g/3½ oz. cooked
peeled prawns/shrimp
6 quail's eggs, hard-
boiled cooked, cooled,
shelled and halved
salt and freshly ground
black pepper

SERVES 4

Cook the asparagus in boiling water until just tender; drain and chop into 2-cm/¾-inch pieces.

Cook the potatoes separately in boiling, salted water until tender; drain and slice.

Mix together the mayonnaise, crème fraîche, olive oil and tarragon leaves. Season with freshly ground black pepper. Toss together the warm potato slices and the mayonnaise dressing.

Flake the brown and white crab meat from the dressed crab. Gently fold the crab meat, prawns/shrimp, quail's eggs and asparagus into the potato salad. Serve at once.

# ANCHOVY POTATO CROQUETTES WITH SALSA VERDE

These small, light-textured, crisp-coated potato croquettes are very hard to resist! The anchovies add a distinctive saltiness to them, making them ideal to serve as a nibble with drinks for a social gathering.

700 g/24½ oz. floury potatoes, peeled and chopped
25 g/1½ tablespoons butter
2 egg yolks, lightly beaten
1 teaspoon anchovy paste
5 anchovy fillets in olive oil, drained and cut into small pieces
salt and freshly ground black pepper

SALSA VERDE
200 g/7 oz. parsley leaves, chopped
15 g/1 cup mint leaves, chopped
1 garlic clove, crushed
2 tablespoons capers, chopped
2 anchovy fillets in olive oil
150 ml/scant ⅔ cup extra virgin olive oil

COATING
flour, for dusting
2 eggs, beaten
dry breadcrumbs or fine matzo meal, for coating
vegetable or sunflower oil, for deep-frying

MAKES 26 CROQUETTES

Cook the potatoes in boiling, salted water until tender; drain. Return the potatoes to the saucepan and cook over a low heat for 2 minutes to dry them off.

Remove from direct heat, add in the butter and mash well, seasoning with freshly ground black pepper. Add in the egg yolks, anchovy paste and anchovy fillets and mix in thoroughly using a wooden spoon.

Spread the mixture out in a layer in a tray, cool, cover and chill for at least 4 hours or overnight.

Make the salsa verde by blending together the parsley, mint, garlic, capers and anchovies into a paste. Add the olive oil and blend to form a textured sauce, seasoning with salt and freshly ground black pepper.

With lightly floured hands and working on a lightly floured surface, shape the chilled potato mixture into 26 small oval-shaped croquettes.

Fill a large, deep pan one-third full of oil for deep-frying. Heat the oil over medium heat until very hot.

Working in batches, for coating, dip the croquettes in the beaten egg, then coat in breadcrumbs or matzo meal. Fry in batches in the hot oil until golden brown on all sides. Remove with a slotted spoon and drain on paper towels. Serve at once, while warm, with the salsa verde.

# GOOSE FAT ROAST POTATOES

Cooking potatoes in goose fat is a simple but effective way of ensuring glorious roasties! Serve these with roast beef or lamb or chicken for a Sunday family meal or a dinner party with friends.

**1 kg/35 oz. potatoes**
**2 tablespoons goose fat**
salt

SERVES 6

Preheat the oven to 220°C (425°F) Gas 7.

Peel the potatoes and, depending on their size, cut them into quarters or halves; you want them to be evenly sized in order to ensure even cooking.

Bring a large pan of salted water to the boil. Add in the potatoes and par-boil for 10 minutes. Drain them thoroughly, return to the pan and shake them in the pan to roughen their surfaces.

Add the goose fat to a roasting pan, place in the preheated oven and heat through so that the fat melts and becomes very hot.

Add the potato chunks to the hot goose fat, tossing and turning them so as to coat them evenly in it, season with salt, and roast in the preheated oven for around 40–45 minutes until golden brown on all sides, turning now and then to ensure even browning. Serve at once.

# NEW POTATOES WITH SOURED CREAM AND LUMPFISH CAVIAR

The salty crunch of lumpfish caviar, together with the slightly sour tang of soured/sour cream, goes well with the mild flavour and smooth texture of new potatoes. Serve these as a delicious nibble for a party.

**12 even-sized new potatoes**
**150 ml/scant ⅔ cup soured/sour cream**
**50 g/2 oz. black lumpfish caviar**
**salt**
**finely chopped chives, to garnish**

MAKES 24

Cook the potatoes in boiling salted water until just tender; drain, cool and pat dry.

Halve each potato lengthways.

Top each potato half with a teaspoon of soured/sour cream and a little lumpfish caviar. Garnish each one with a small pinch of chopped chives. Serve at once.

# TRUFFLE MASH

This smooth-textured mashed potato with its subtle truffle flavour is a treat, managing to be at once rich, yet light. Serve it with grilled/broiled steak or roast beef or roast chicken for a sophisticated meal.

800 g/28 oz. floury
    potatoes, peeled and
    chopped
100 g/7 tablespoons
    cold butter, cubed
1 teaspoon truffle oil
salt and freshly ground
    black pepper

SERVES 4

Cook the potatoes in boiling, salted water until tender; drain.

Place a potato ricer over a pan and pass the freshly drained potatoes through it. Alternatively, mash the potatoes thoroughly using a potato masher.

Add in the butter a few cubes at a time and, using a fork, fold into the potato. Season with salt and freshly ground black pepper. Add the truffle oil and fold in well. Serve at once.

# CLASSIC POTATO GRATIN

This classic French way of cooking potatoes is always a treat
to eat. The combination of yielding potato, coated in a rich, creamy
sauce, is very pleasurable indeed. It's an excellent accompaniment
to roast lamb or a rich dish of beef braised in red wine and also
a luxurious vegetarian dish in its own right.

300 ml/1¼ cups
  double/heavy cream
300 ml/1¼ cups milk
4 tablespoons fresh
  thyme leaves
1 garlic clove, crushed
freshly grated nutmeg
1 kg/35 oz. waxy
  potatoes
40 g/3 tablespoons
  butter
2 shallots, finely
  chopped
salt and freshly ground
  black pepper

SERVES 6

Preheat the oven to 180°C (350°F) Gas 4.

Place the cream, milk, thyme and garlic in a pan and season with
freshly grated nutmeg, salt and freshly ground black pepper. Bring
to the boil, then remove from the heat and set aside to infuse.

Peel and then slice the potatoes very thinly lengthways; using a
mandoline to slice them speeds up the process, but they can be
sliced by hand. Place them in a bowl of cold water, set aside for
15 minutes, then drain and pat the potato slices dry.

Use 15 g/1 tablespoon of the butter to generously grease an
ovenproof dish.

Layer the potato slices in the dish, sprinkling each layer with a little
of the chopped shallots and seasoning well with salt and freshly
ground black pepper. Finish with a layer of potato slices.

Bring the infused milk back to boiling point and then pour it over
the potatoes.

Melt the remaining butter and brush over the top layer of potatoes.

Bake in the preheated oven for 1½ hours until the potatoes are
tender and the top is golden brown. Serve at once.

# RICH BEEF AND POTATO STEW

There is always something very heartening about a stew. In this recipe, succulent whole shallots and tender potatoes are an excellent counterfoil for soft chunks of tasty beef. Serve it with a green vegetable, such as buttered cabbage, kale or cavolo nero.

700 g/24½ oz. braising beef steak, cut into 2.5 cm/1 inch cubes
50 g/2 oz. dried porcini slices
3 tablespoons extra virgin olive oil
8 shallots, peeled
1 celery stalk, thinly sliced
1 bay leaf
3 sprigs of thyme
300 ml/1¼ cups red wine
500 ml/2 cups plus 2 tablespoons chicken or beef stock
1 tablespoon tomato purée/paste
1 garlic clove, chopped
12 small, even-sized waxy potatoes or 6 large waxy potatoes, halved
salt and freshly ground black pepper

SERVES 4

De-chill the braising beef steak by removing it from the fridge 30 minutes before cooking. Soak the dried porcini in hot water for 30 minutes.

Preheat the oven to 150°C (300°F) Gas 2.

Heat 2 tablespoons of the olive oil in an ovenproof/flameproof casserole dish. Fry the beef in batches until browned on all sides; remove and reserve.

Add the remaining olive oil to the casserole dish and heat through over a medium heat. Add in the shallots, celery, bay leaf and thyme and fry, stirring, for 3–5 minutes until the shallots are lightly browned.

Pour in the red wine, bring to the boil and cook briskly, uncovered, for 5 minutes to reduce it slightly. Add in the reserved beef, stock, tomato purée/paste and garlic, mixing well. Season with salt and freshly ground black pepper.

Bring to the boil, then cover and cook in the preheated oven for 1 hour.

Add in the garlic and whole potatoes, bring back to the boil on the hob/stovetop, then cover and return to the oven to cook for a further 30 minutes, until the potatoes are tender. Serve at once.

# SAFFRON MASH FISH PIES

Adding saffron to the mashed potato topping gives both colour and flavour. As they can be prepared in advance and then baked in the oven, these pretty fish pies are perfect for dinner party entertaining.

500 ml/2 cups plus 2 tablespoons fish stock

400 g/14 oz. white fish fillet, skinned, chopped into 3-cm/1¼-inch cubes

400 g/14 oz. salmon fillet, skinned, chopped into 3-cm/1¼-inch cubes

1.5 kg/3 lb. 5 oz. floury potatoes, peeled and chopped into chunks

100 ml/⅓ cup double/ heavy cream

1 teaspoon saffron strands, finely ground

50 g/3 tablespoons butter

1 tablespoon olive oil

1 leek, finely chopped

1 fennel bulb, finely chopped

50 ml/3½ tablespoons dry white wine

40 g/heaping ¼ cup plain/all-purpose flour

2 tablespoons finely chopped parsley

grated zest of ½ lemon

squeeze of lemon juice

100 g/3½ oz. cooked peeled prawns/shrimp

salt and freshly ground black pepper

SERVES 6

Bring the fish stock to the boil in a large saucepan. Add in the fish cubes and simmer for 2–3 minutes until just cooked through. Remove with a slotted spoon and set aside to cool, reserving the stock.

Cook the potatoes in boiling, salted water until tender; drain. While the potatoes are cooking, heat the double/heavy cream and saffron in a small pan, bring to the boil, then remove from the heat.

Add 25 g/1½ tablespoons of the butter and the hot saffron cream to the potatoes and mash together well. Season with salt and freshly ground black pepper. Set aside.

Heat the olive oil in a frying pan/skillet. Gently fry the leek and fennel for 3 minutes until softened. Add the white wine and cook for 2–3 minutes until the wine is reduced and syrupy. Season with salt and freshly ground black pepper. Set aside.

Heat the remaining butter in a heavy-based saucepan until melted. Stir in the flour and cook, stirring, for 2 minutes. Gradually mix in the reserved fish stock. Cook, stirring, until the mixture comes to the boil and thickens to form a sauce. Season with salt and freshly ground black pepper. Stir in the parsley and lemon zest and juice.

Preheat the oven to 200°C (400°F) Gas 6.

Gently fold together the poached fish, prawns/shrimp, fried leek mixture and sauce. Divide between four small pie dishes, spreading it across the base. Top each one with an even layer of the saffron mash. Bake the pies in the preheated oven for 25–30 minutes until piping hot and lightly browned. Alternatively, to make one large pie, spread the mixture in the base of an ovenproof dish, top with the saffron mash and bake in the preheated oven for 40 minutes until piping hot and lightly browned. Serve at once.

# POTATO-STUFFED ROAST DUCK

A light-textured potato stuffing contrasts nicely with the richness
of the duck. Serve the roast duck with vegetables, such as green beans
or peas and honey-glazed carrots and a rich red wine or port gravy
for a splendid roast meal.

a 1.2-kg/2½-lbs. duck
400 g/14 oz. floury
   potatoes, peeled and
   chopped
1 tablespoon olive oil
1 onion, finely chopped
1 garlic clove, chopped
3 tablespoons freshly
   chopped sage leaves
salt and freshly ground
   black pepper

SERVES 4

De-chill the duck by removing it from the fridge for 30 minutes
before cooking.

Preheat the oven to 200°C (400°F) Gas 6.

Cook the potatoes in salted boiling water until tender; drain and
return to the pan. Meanwhile, heat the olive oil in a frying pan/
skillet. Add in the onion and fry gently for 5 minutes, stirring now
and then, until softened. Add in the garlic and fry for 2 minutes,
stirring often, until fragrant.

Add the fried onion mixture, together with its oil, to the drained
potatoes, mashing together well. Season with salt and freshly
ground black pepper. Mix in the chopped sage.

Season the duck with salt and freshly ground black pepper
and prick the skin on its breast. Fill the duck cavity with the
potato mixture.

Place the duck on a rack in a roasting pan. Roast in the preheated
oven for 1½ hours until cooked through. Serve at once.

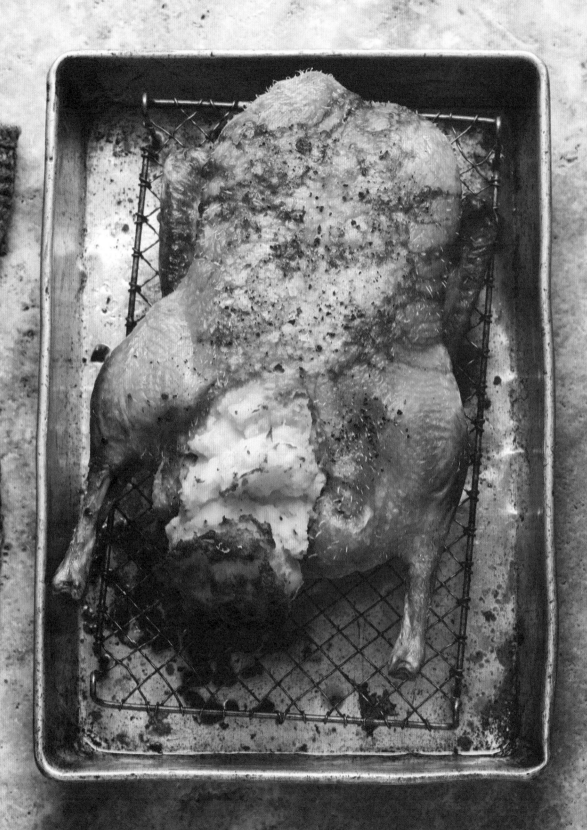

# INDEX

apples: apple sauce 90
  potato, apple and onion
    hash 77

bacon: mushroom bacon
  potato dumplings 64
baked potatoes, stuffed 85
beans: potato bean
  quesadillas 121
beef: rich beef and potato
  stew 152
boulangere potatoes 52
bubble and squeak, kale 82

caldo verde 51
carrots: potato, sweet potato
  and carrot dhal 129
cauliflower potato curry 109
chaat masala, potato 130
chard: chickpea, chard and
  potato stew 56
cheese: cheesy three-root
  bake 67
  potato, cheese and chive
    pierogi 93
  potato cheese pie 101
  potato cheese scones 55
chicken: Malaysian chicken
  and potato curry 125
  stoved chicken 63
chickpeas: chickpea, chard
  and potato stew 56
  potato chaat masala 130
chips, triple-cooked 94
chorizo potato salad 19
chowder, cod, sweetcorn and
  prawn 97

chutney, tamarind 110
crisps, black pepper 15
croquettes, anchovy
  potato 143
curry: cauliflower potato
  curry 109
  Malaysian chicken and
    potato curry 125
  potato chaat masala 130
  potato, sweet potato and
    carrot dhal 129

Danish-style glazed
  potatoes 89
dhal, potato, sweet potato
  and carrot 129
duck, potato-stuffed roast 156
dumplings: mushroom bacon
  potato dumplings 64
  potato, cheese and chive
    pierogi 93

eggs: Spanish potato
  tortilla 35

fish: anchovy potato
  croquettes 143
  baked seabass on herbed
    potatoes 68
  griddled tuna niçoise 20
  Jansson's temptation 98
  saffron mash fish pies 155
  salmon fishcakes with
    watercress sauce 36
  Swedish-style herring and
    potato salad 16
French potato salad 12

gado-gado 31
gardener's pie 59
gnocchi, potato 78
gratin, classic potato 151
green beans: pesto, potato and
  green bean linguine 32

harissa potato and lentil
  salad 39
hash, potato, apple and
  onion 77
hash browns 74
hasselback potatoes with
  Parma ham 81
herbs: herbed crushed
  potatoes 47
  salsa verde 143
hotpot, Lancashire 86

Indian five-spice sautéed
  potatoes 114

Jansson's temptation 98

kale: caldo verde 51
  kale bubble and squeak 82
kimchi potato cakes 118

lamb: Lancashire hotpot 86
leeks: chilled leek and potato
  soup 28
lentils: harissa potato and
  lentil salad 39
  potato, sweet potato and
    carrot dhal 129
lumpfish caviar, new potatoes
  with soured cream and 147

Malaysian chicken and potato curry 125

mashed potato: saffron mash fish pies 155

truffle mash 148

Mediterranean mussel potato soup 27

mint salsa, new potatoes with 23

miso potato soup 60

mushroom bacon potato dumplings 64

mussels: Mediterranean mussel potato soup 27

onions: potato, apple and onion hash 77

pakoras, potato coriander 122

pancakes, parsley potato 90

pancetta: sauteed potatoes with pancetta and garlic 44

Parma ham, hasselback potatoes with 81

pasta: pesto, potato and green bean linguine 32

Persian-style saffron rice with potatoes 136

pesto, potato and green bean linguine 32

pierogi, potato, cheese and chive 93

pies: potato cheese pie 101

saffron mash fish pies 155

piquant potato straws 106

potato cakes, kimchi 118

prawns: cod, sweetcorn and prawn chowder 97

raita, potato 24

rice, Persian-style saffron 136

roast potatoes: goose fat roast potatoes 144

rosemary garlic potatoes 139

zahtar roast potatoes 126

saffron mash fish pies 155

salads: chorizo potato salad 19

French potato salad 12

gado-gado 31

griddled tuna niçoise 20

harissa potato and lentil salad 39

seafood new potato salad 140

Swedish-style herring and potato salad 16

salsa, mint 23

salsa verde 143

samosas, potato 110

scones, potato cheese 55

seafood new potato salad 140

seaweed butter potatoes 48

soups: caldo verde 51

chilled leek and potato soup 28

cod, sweetcorn and prawn chowder 97

Mediterranean mussel potato soup 27

miso potato soup 60

Spanish potato tortilla 35

stews: chickpea, chard and potato stew 56

rich beef and potato stew 152

stoved chicken 63

straws, piquant potato 106

Swedish-style herring and potato salad 16

sweet potatoes: potato, sweet potato and carrot dhal 129

sweetcorn: cod, sweetcorn and prawn chowder 97

tamarind chutney 110

tomatoes: piquant tomato sauce 78

romesco sauce 113

tortillas: potato bean quesadillas 121

Spanish potato tortilla 35

truffle mash 148

turmeric potato wraps 117

watercress sauce, salmon fishcakes with 36

wedges, potato 113

wraps, turmeric potato 117

yogurt: potato raita 24

# ACKNOWLEDGEMENTS

Many thanks to Cindy Richards and Julia Charles for commissioning this book on a wonderful but unsung ingredient. It's always a pleasure to work with the team at Ryland, Peters and Small. RPS are known for their beautiful cookbooks and I'm thrilled with how this one looks. Thank you, Clare Winfield, for your elegant photography, Sonya Nathoo for your design and David Hearn for your work as Production Controller. Many thanks, also, to Julia Charles and Miriam Catley for their work editing the book.

My thanks for their time to Lucy Carroll of Carroll's Heritage Potatoes, John Garton of Genuine Jersey Products Association, and David Little of the Little Organic Farm. Recipe testing requires tasters, so thanks to my family and friends for their help with this, especially my husband Chris.

## PICTURE CREDITS

All photography by Clare Winfield apart from:
10l Hughes Herve/hemis.fr/Getty Images
10r Jim Richardson/Getty Images
11l MAIKA 777/Getty Images
11c Christian Declercq/Getty Images
11r Nariner Nanu/AFP/Getty Images
42l Michael S. Lewis/Getty Images
42r Laura Berman/Visuals Unlimited, Inc./ Getty Images
43 Tastyart Ltd Rob White/Getty Images
72l Steve Painter/Ryland, Peters & Small
72r Steve Painter/Ryland, Peters & Small
73l Westend61/Getty Images
73r Steve Painter/Ryland, Peters & Small
104l Steve Painter/Ryland, Peters & Small
104r Christian Kober/Getty Images
105 India Picture/UIG/Getty Images
134l Clare Lewington
134r Clare Lewington
135 Gavin Kingcome Photography/Getty Images